# Tray Gourmet:

## Be Your Own Chef in the College Cafeteria

Also by Larry Berger:

**UP YOUR SCORE:**
**THE UNDERGROUND GUIDE TO PSYCHING OUT THE S.A.T.**
(With Manek Mistry and Paul Rossi)

# Tray GOURMET

## BE YOUR OWN CHEF IN THE COLLEGE CAFETERIA

### Larry Berger + Lynn Harris

THE Original COLLEGE CAFETERIA COOKBOOK

illustrated by Chris Kalb

Lake Isle Press, Inc. • New York

To our parents and grandparents with love and thanks.


Florence and Toby Berger
Doris and Henry Berger
Belle and Joseph Cohen


Florence and James Harris
Lucy and Charles Harris
Libby and Hyman Warshawsky


Shirley and Bill Kalb
Maude and Wilbur Kalb
Eva and Gilbert Hanson

A portion of the authors' proceeds will be donated to the Children's Defense Fund.

If you would like information about how your campus organization, team, or club can use this book as a fund-raiser, please contact Lake Isle Press, Inc., 2095 Broadway, Suite 404, New York, New York 10023. Phone: 212-769-2361.

# *Acknowledgments*

## Thanks to

Our Yale friends who inspired us to write this cookbook and who will inspire us always.

Special thanks to those who shared cooking tips and survived a battery of taste tests: Mark Badger, Andrew Berger, Daniel Berger, Debbie Bloom, Melody Brown, Melissa Burkhart, Alison Buttenheim, Claudio Cambon, James Chang, Ethan Cohen, Steve Cohen, Jeff Dolven, Amy Doyle, Gavin Edwards, Amelia Eisch, Dan Etheridge, Harriet Fennell, Eva Festa, David Franklin, Paola Freccero, Allegra Growdon, Kate Guiney, Jeff Hadler, James Hannaham, Matt Heimer, Jason Jacobs, Paul Jamieson, Michael Jasny, Mark Kautz, Dana Kelly, Paula Kenefick, Chris Kincade, Andy Lee, Theo Liebmann, Colin Lingle, Dahlia Lithwick, Meg Marshall, Kevin Mayes, Andrew Michaelson, Kent Pekel, Jim Ponichtera, Anne Robinson, Claudia Rosen, Jim Rosenfeld, Cris Rothfuss, Paul Saint-Amour, Glenn Sanchez, Jenna Sellars, Zach Silverstein, Fred Singer, the women of Something Extra, Ann Song, Ed Spitzberg, Leah Strigler, Duncan Thieme, Gillian Thomas, Cindy Toth, Brian Watt, Mike Warren, Allison Wegner, Jay Withgott, Jim Wroth, and Dena Wyner.

The Winsor '86 Women who helped with our research:

Katie Beatty, Alexis Broome, Lynne Cohen, Sarah Daley, Cindy Green, Page Higgins, Marjorie Just, Jennifer McCullen, Dana Osborn, Margaret Otte ('84), Emily Perlman, Anne Seiler, Kim Shapiro, Liz Tennican, Angel Uhlmann, Kathy Vatter, Pam Webb, and Connie Wong.

Friends at other colleges who helped with our research:

Jill Condelli, Kirsten Evans, Randy Faigin, Mike Gonik, Adam Grace, Glenn Greenberg, Steve Levitsky, David Schwartz, Jared Strote, Nancy Tobin, Robin Turner, Stephanie Turner, Todd Walker, and Ken Wood.

The National Association of College and University Food Services, for their interest and for their help in funding this project.

The friendly, helpful people of Yale University Dining Halls for providing our test kitchens and photo studio, and for making food that is (shhh!) actually pretty good.

Special thanks to:

Calhoun College: Mabel Barnes, Sophie Cweirtniewicz, Milton Flaks, Willie Ford, Willie Foskey, Lostina Lee, Mary Mahoney, Josephine Matthews, David Mendez, LaVerne Miley, Mildred Moore, and Annette Tracey.

Silliman College: Julia Aranjo, Mike Aaronian, Evelyn Belfort, Maureen Carbone, Stuart Comon, Craig Conyers, Jimmy Conyers, Sylvia Conyers, Phil Czekala, Dan Ernst, Phil Floyd, Mary Gammon, Sheryl Groth, Teddy Jackson, Howard Krom, Peggy Nelson, and Ralph Salemme.

And all the friendly folks at the Alternative Food Line.

## Thanks also to

Lynn's American Society of Magazine Editors roommates, fellow interns, and editors for their ideas and enthusiasm.

Belle Cohen for being our chief researcher and public relations consultant.

Wendy Crisp of New Chapter Press for her encouragement.

Anita Diamant for her generous and sound advice.

Katie Hackett for the Swahili in the Coffee with Milk recipe.

Eric Liftin and Andrew Reich for coming up with the title.

Jim and Elizabeth Mandell for their love, support, and hospitality.

Judy Mandell for her publishing counsel.

The MIT Office of the Dean for Undergraduate Education for their patience and support throughout the publication process.

Naples Pizza and Restaurant for their cinnamon toast recipe and for being there when we needed them.

The Boston chapter of the National Organization for Women for their flexibility, enthusiasm, and sisterhood.

Rabbi James Ponet of Yale Hillel for his exceptional enthusiasm.

Rita Rosenkranz, our faithful, insightful, and gracious agent, who makes great pecan bread.

Jane Ross and Hiroko Kiiffner of Lake Isle Press for the vision, expertise, and enthusiasm they have dedicated to this project.

Mary Tabacchi, Professor of Food Chemistry and Nutrition at the Cornell University School of Hotel and Restaurant Administration, for sharing her nutrition erudition.

The Ten O'Clock News gang of summer '88 for their ideas: Chris Lydon, Tom Brendler, Amy Gilburg, Kathia Manzi, Lynn Mason, Phil McNamara, and David Rohde.

The women of the Warner Building (Annie, Jenny, Kris, and Laura) for letting us write in their pad.

The women of 10 Wyatt (Lynn Festa and Juliet Siler) for sharing midnight quesadillas; for contributing to a stable, distraction-free working environment; and for convincing no one that food is for nourishment, not for pleasure.

Lynn's family and friends in Barcelona, Montclair, and Mexico for their inspiration, culinary and otherwise.

Montgomery Publishing and *Today's Spirit* for their computers and their patience, and for their slow summer which ensured that Chris could get this done on time.

# Contents

# ForeWORD

"Mmmmm! This is good. You guys should write a cookbook."
— *too many people to mention them all by name*

The cafeteria food of the past—mystery meat, mystery meat with brown sauce, brown sauce with brown sauce—left hungry college students with limited means for survival. Back then, you had three options: (**1**) close your eyes and eat fast, (**2**) order a large pizza, or (**3**) pray for a care package. But today's college cafeterias have given students a fourth option—we call it "cafeteria cooking." Now that microwaves, salad bars, toasters, and a wealth of other cooking resources are standard in the cafeteria, college students across the country have begun to cook their own delicious meals **using only ingredients and supplies already provided in the cafeteria**: no shopping, no dishwashing, no illegal dorm room hotpots.

*Tray Gourmet: Be Your Own Chef in the College Cafeteria* is the very first collection of cafeteria recipes. It is a product of popular demand. During our first year in college, word began to spread about our experiments with cafeteria cuisine. Crowds of students would form as we used cream, butter, cheese, herbs, and the microwave to transform a boring plate of plain cafeteria pasta into a mouth-watering Fettucine Alfredo. They watched us convert everyday beef into scrumptious steak teriyaki, and make colorful, creative salads from the fixings at the salad bar. They watched us make cheese and chocolate fondues from scratch, with enough forks for everyone to share. With their mouths still full, they gratefully offered to write our term papers and insisted that we write a cafeteria cookbook.

The recipes in this cookbook represent many semesters of intensive experimentation and nationwide research. In addition to our own recipes, we've included cafeteria recipes from our classmates and from students at colleges across the country.

With *Tray Gourmet* as your guide, you can be a cafeteria chef even if back home you always burned the salad. So grab *Tray Gourmet,* grab your friends, and prepare a twenty-course cafeteria banquet. These could be the best courses you'll ever have in college.

**IMPORTANT NOTICE TO PARENTS: The authors in no way mean to imply that ownership of *Tray Gourmet* by your child should cause you to interrupt or discontinue your regular care package schedule.**

# INTRODUCTION
## TO CAFETERIA COOKING

## Cafeteria Cooking 101:
## Basic Information

### Improvising and Substituting

We created a lot of the recipes in this book by improvising. We would toss a few likely ingredients together, taste the results, add a little of this, taste, add a little of that, and taste, until we had perfected a recipe that was worthy of *Tray Gourmet*. We recommend that you do the same. If you love Brussels sprouts and have happened to notice the slight anti-Brussels sprout bias of this book, then by all means try including them in one of our recipes. Or if an ingredient called for in one of our recipes is not available in your cafeteria, try substituting something similar.

### Getting What You Need

If your cafeteria lacks an ingredient called for in a recipe, take action. Talk to one of the cafeteria managers. Say, for example, "I think it would be great if you could offer olive oil at the salad bar. It's terrific for salad dressings and it's better for you than most other oils." Or write a note to this effect and put it in the suggestion box. Cafeterias often have suggestion boxes, and the cafeteria managers we talked to said that they are extremely eager to respond to good suggestions, but their suggestion boxes are usually empty. Someday soon, suggestion boxes across the country will be teeming with creative suggestions from the readers of *Tray Gourmet*.

### Yield

Unless otherwise noted, the recipes in this book yield enough for one person, possibly with seconds. If you want to make more, increase the amount of each ingredient proportionately and cook longer. Doubling the recipe doesn't necessarily require doubling the cooking time—follow the directions according to how the food should look when it's done.

**11**

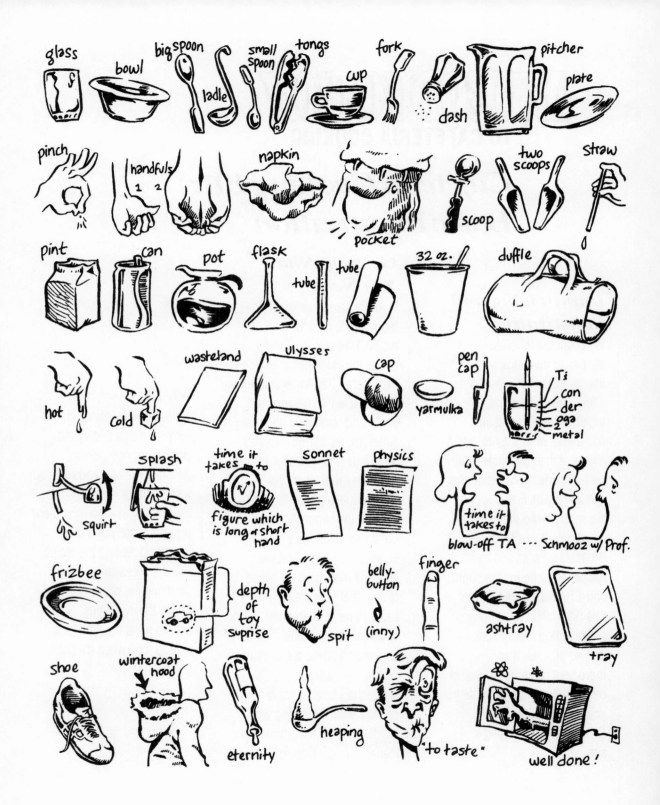

# *Soupspoons and Handfuls:*
# *Measuring in the Cafeteria*

There are many fun things to measure in a college cafeteria. You can measure the density of the sneeze guard on the salad bar. You can measure how deep a meatball will sink when submerged in a bowl of yogurt. You can propel pats of butter to the ceiling with a spoon and then calculate the average time required for the butter to unstick onto your classmates. Unfortunately, this section will be of no help to you should you desire to engage in such activities. It will, however, help you to understand the measurements that we use in this cookbook. Ours are not standard cooking measurements because college cafeterias do not have standard measuring equipment. The sizes of the utensils listed below may vary from cafeteria to cafeteria, but don't worry about it. Precise measurements are not necessary for our recipes.

## *Our measurements are:*

| | |
|---|---|
| **Dash** | The amount that emerges from one brisk shake of a salt or pepper shaker. |
| **Teaspoon** | The smaller of the two spoon sizes offered in your cafeteria, filled to the top of the spoon. |
| | ***Note:*** *Assume that 1 plastic packet of ketchup, mustard, or mayonnaise equals 1 teaspoon.* |
| **Soupspoon** | The larger of the two spoon sizes offered in your cafeteria, filled to the top of the spoon. |
| **Heaping Teaspoon** or **Heaping Soupspoon** | As much as the spoon can hold. |
| **Handful** | As much as you can hold in a clean hand. |
| **Cup** | One coffee cup filled nearly to the top. |
| **Glass** | One soda or juice glass filled nearly to the top (usually slightly taller than a cup). |
| **Bowl** | A soup bowl filled nearly to the top but not heaped over the top. |
| **Pat** | One square of butter. |

## *Helpful Hints*

• **We know that cafeteria glassware does not come with handy lines drawn on it for measuring fractions like "2/3 glass." Just eyeball these fractions.**
• **In order to measure spoonfuls of fruit juice from a dispenser, dispense the juice into a cup or glass first and measure from there.**
• **You probably don't need us to tell you this, but you are less likely to lose your cafeteria privileges if you measure out handfuls by spooning ingredients into your hand (as opposed to plunging your hand into the salad bar).**

# *Know Nukes:*
# *Using the Microwave*

*Microwave ovens are like snowflakes. A large blizzard of them could mean canceled classes. And, of course, no two microwaves are alike. The ovens will vary from school to school depending on their wattage and how often they are used. 30 seconds on High in Colby's microwave might leave a brownie chilly; 30 seconds on High in Colorado State's microwave might cause a violent chocolate explosion.*

*To be on the safe side, our microwave instructions are qualitative rather than quantitative. We'll say "microwave until the cheese melts" or "microwave until mushrooms are hot" rather than provide an exact cooking time. You may have to open the door a few times during cooking to check on the progress of your recipe. Be sure to restart the microwave after you close the door.*

**IMPORTANT NOTE: All of the cooking instructions in our recipes assume that the microwave is set on High.**

## Helpful Hints

• Some microwaves have "hot spots," certain areas on your food that may cook faster than others. If your food tends to warm unevenly, stir it or rotate the plate during cooking.

• The more food there is in the microwave, the longer it will take to heat. If a recipe calls for heating two different foods, it might be faster to heat one item at a time than to make the microwave use its energy on two things at once.

• If you are microwaving bread or one of its relatives—muffins, bagels, danishes, etc.— place a napkin underneath it to keep it from getting soggy.

## Dramatic Explosions as Attention-Getters

The following are things you should never, ever put in a microwave:

• a whole egg in its shell, raw or hard-boiled

• a whole hard-boiled egg without its shell (cut it in halves or quarters instead)

• a poached, fried, or baked egg unless you have pierced the outer membrane of the yolk several times with a fork or knife

• a frankfurter, baked potato, or any other food with a skin, unless you have pierced it several times with a fork or knife

• anything metal, including aluminum foil

15

# Proposing a Toast: Using the Toaster Oven

Some cafeterias have toaster ovens in addition to, or instead of, microwaves. By "toaster oven," we do not mean those big rotary appliances that roll the bread under the burners and out onto the bottom tray. Toaster ovens are small ovens in which you can toast or bake food. While we usually give microwave directions, many recipes, such as pizzas and burgers, can be prepared in a toaster oven instead. The only problem with toaster ovens, as far as our recipes are concerned, is that you can't put plates or bowls in them. Just use your judgment. Place any potentially messy food on aluminum foil (ask the cafeteria manager). If your cafeteria has both microwave and toaster ovens, we recommend using the microwave for all recipes except those with bread as the main ingredient—bread stays crisper in a toaster oven.

# Substitute Teachers: Lower Calorie Alternatives

Cafeteria cooking can help you avoid the greasier, more fattening, and less nutritious institutional meals. For those eaters seeking to avoid "the freshperson fifteen," "the sophomore spare tire," and other forms of collegiate weight gain, we have indicated instances where you can make recipes somewhat less caloric by substituting a lower calorie ingredient. You can, for example, use plain yogurt instead of sour cream, cut down on the sugar, or bag the butter altogether.

For more about nutrition and health, see page 181.

# the RECIPES

# REASONS
## to get out of bed
### Great Breakfasts

Our delicious breakfast recipes serve two important academic purposes: (*1*) they will tempt you to get out of bed, which, as clinical tests have shown, significantly increases your chances of going to class, and (*2*) once you get to class, the good breakfast in your system will help you stay awake.

Be sure to see page 168 for how to squeeze your own fresh orange or grapefruit juice.

*A hearty breakfast for chilly Dartmouth mornings.*

**2** English muffin **halves**
**2** **pats** butter
**1** plain omelette, 1 fried egg (over well), or 1 serving scrambled eggs
**1** **slice** ham, 2 strips bacon, or 2 sausage links
**1** **slice** cheese or 1 handful shredded cheese, any kind

Toast the English muffin and butter it while still hot. Place the egg on one half. Top with ham, bacon, or sausage, and then with cheese. Toast or microwave until the cheese melts. Before microwaving a fried egg, make sure to pierce the outer membrane of the yolk several times with a fork.

# Passionate French Toasting

This is something you'll want in your mouth. Put any of the 3 following toppings on French toast (or waffles).

## • Apple Topping

| | |
|---|---|
| **1** | apple, sliced thin (also good with bananas, pears, or peaches) |
| **2** | **pats** butter |
| **2** | **teaspoons** lemon or orange juice |
| | Cinnamon sugar (see page 29) |
| **1 or 2** | **slices** French toast |
| | Maple syrup, heated in the microwave (optional) |

Put fruit slices in a bowl with butter, juice, and cinnamon sugar. Microwave until butter melts and mixture is hot. Stir until fruit slices are covered with the sauce. Pour fruit mixture over French toast. Add maple syrup or sprinkle cinnamon sugar on top, if you like.

## • Peach Topping

Make the above recipe with peaches, substitute a dash of ginger for the cinnamon, and sprinkle granola over the top.

• Spread any of the *Je Ne Sais Quoi Crêpe* fillings (page 24) on French toast.

# Je Ne Sais Quoi Crêpes

*This recipe turns dull cafeteria pancakes into elegant French crêpes.*

**1** of *Les Fillings* from the following recipes
**3** pancakes

Prepare the filling of your choice (see the following). Spread the filling on each pancake and carefully roll pancakes up with the filling inside (secure with toothpick if necessary). Arrange the pancakes side by side on a plate and garnish with fruit slices, if you like.

## Les Fillings:

### • A l'Orange

**2** **pats** butter
**1/3** **bowl** plain yogurt
**2** **soupspoons** orange juice
**2** **soupspoons** sugar or honey

Put the butter in a bowl and melt in microwave. Add yogurt, juice, and sugar or honey and stir until smooth.

### • Au Peanutte

**2** **soupspoons** cream cheese
**2** **soupspoons** peanut butter
**2** **soupspoons** milk
**1** **soupspoon** honey
**Small handful** Grape Nuts (optional)

Combine cream cheese and peanut butter in bowl. Microwave together until soft enough to stir. Add milk and honey; stir until well blended. Add Grape Nuts, if you like.

## • *Banane Extraordinaire*

**1/3   bowl** cream cheese
**2 or 3   pats** butter
**1**   banana, sliced crosswise into thin circles
Cinnamon sugar (see page 29)

Soften cream cheese and butter together in the microwave. Stir together thoroughly. Spread the mixture on the pancakes and place the sliced bananas on top of the spread. Sprinkle on cinnamon sugar to taste.

## • *Avec Crème de Maple*

**2   soupspoons** maple syrup
**2   soupspoons** cream cheese or plain yogurt

Add syrup to cream cheese. Microwave until soft. Stir thoroughly.

# ome Like It Hot

*"This porridge is
just right."*
—Goldilocks

1 **cup** milk (or enough to cover the cereal in
the bowl)

1/2 **bowl** Grape Nuts or granola, or a
combination of the two

**Any** of the following: 1 pat butter, 1 sliced
banana, 1 teaspoon sugar, 1 teaspoon brown
sugar, 1 teaspoon honey, 1 handful raisins, 1
soupspoon peanut butter

Pour the milk over the cereal. Add any of the optional
ingredients. Microwave until the milk starts to bubble and
the butter (if included) melts. Stir well. If it's too hot to eat,
add a little cold milk.

# A Full Page of Spreads

*Try these creative spreads on two warm bagel halves, two slices of toast, or a toasted English muffin.*

- Put 5 or 6 pats of butter in a cup and let soften for a few minutes (you might want to place it near the toaster, but don't let it melt). Add 1 teaspoon honey and stir diligently with a fork until the honey and butter are thoroughly blended. Spread on toast.
- Spread cream cheese on toast. Place a few peach or apple slices on top, and sprinkle with cinnamon.
- Spread peanut butter on toast and top with banana slices and raisins.
- Spread toast with peanut butter and then with your choice of jam or jelly. Microwave or toast until hot.
- Butter untoasted bread. Mix 1 soupspoon orange juice with 1 soupspoon brown sugar. Spoon onto bread. Microwave or toast until spread starts to bubble.

# Cinnamon Toast Like They Make it at Naples

*Naples Pizza restaurant in New Haven (90 Wall St.) is to Yalies as Arnold's is to the "Happy Days" gang. Pizza notwithstanding, Naples makes the best cinnamon toast in the whole world. Here's what happened when we went to get their recipe.*

LYNN: Hi, Lynette, I'm writing a cookbook and—

LYNETTE: (everyone's favorite waitress): Rice pudding. You want the rice pudding recipe.

LYNN: No, actually, the cinnamon toast.

LYNETTE: Good, because we're not allowed to give out the rice pudding recipe. Everyone wants the rice pudding recipe. About the cinnamon toast, you gotta ask Eddie.

Our adaptation of Eddie's recipe:

**2 soupspoons** cinnamon
**2 soupspoons** powdered sugar
**6 pats** butter
**1 slice** toast

Put all ingredients in a cup and microwave until the butter melts. Stir together and spread ridiculous amounts on your toast.

If powdered sugar is not available, try this (stick to a ratio of 3 parts granulated sugar to 1 part cinnamon):

**1 teaspoon** cinnamon
**3 teaspoons** sugar
**An** empty salt or pepper shaker (transfer contents of half-full shaker to half-empty one)
**Some** generously buttered bread

Mix cinnamon and sugar in a bowl and then spoon mixture into the empty shaker. Sprinkle as much cinnamon sugar as you like over buttered bread. If you don't have a shaker, fill a spoon with the mixture and jiggle it over the bread. Toast or microwave until the butter starts to melt—you'll see it start to darken the cinnamon mixture.

# LIST OF CHARACTERS

- Oatmeal
- Bilbo Baggins
- Sliced Apples
- Cinnamon
- Hester Prynne
- Raisins
- Brown Sugar
- Granola
- Odysseus
- Honey
- Plain or Flavored Yogurt
- Peanut Butter
- Jane Eyre
- Sliced Banana
- Wheat Germ
- Grape Nuts
- Iago
- Pear Slices
- Peach Slices
- Jose Arcadio Buendía

# BRIEF SYNOPSIS

The above characters, propelled by an unseen force, find themselves together in a bowl of bland oatmeal, where they undergo a grueling imprisonment in a microwave oven. The experience forces them to come to terms with themselves, one another, and existence. The unified oatmeal then faces consumption with serenity and triumph.

## Commentary

The entanglement of the ingredients in the oatmeal establishes profound conflicts on several levels, literal and figurative, internal and external. Yet any lasting confrontation among ingredients is ultimately averted; it is the whole of the new oatmeal mixture that takes precedence. Its glorious emergence from the microwave— the womb of technology—can be read as an allegory for the possibility of culinary regeneration and rebirth through technological progress.

Ironically, though, the text leaves the reader to gnaw on an unresolved question: Does this swift progress toward the renewal of the whole actually condemn the individual to an anonymous existence as an old-fashioned oat in a post-modern gruel?

## QUESTIONS FOR REVIEW

1. Treating breakfast as text, analyze the development of Grape Nuts imagery and other cereal allusions throughout the recipe. How does this symbolism help account for the triumph of crunchiness over milk?

2. Using specific examples, discuss the significance of the recipe's shift in point of view from the cook to the oatmeal. How does the reader come to terms with this displacement of human subjectivity?

3. Construct a Freudian interpretation of the recipe, centering on the role of the banana. Apply your interpretation to a personal experience.

Add as much as you like of any combination of ingredients under "List of Characters" to your bowl of plain oatmeal (or any other plain hot cereal). Stir them in. If the oatmeal has cooled, reheat in the microwave. Stir again and taste. The new ingredients should be warm, too—you don't want any cold spots in your hot oatmeal.

Some particularly good combinations are:
- Sliced peaches, brown sugar, and cinnamon
- Granola and fruit-flavored yogurt
- Apples, raisins, and honey

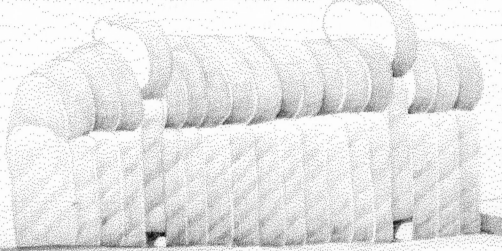

# LOAF STORY
## Sandwich Ideas

Your relationship with cafeteria sandwiches may be getting stale. Maybe it's time for you to start seeing other recipes. Remember, love means never having to say you're hungry.

# Some Sandwich Standbys

Tray Gourmet *never forgets the classics.*

• **Egg Salad Sandwich**

Prepare **Bill and Ted's Eggcellent Salad** (page 56).  Make it into a sandwich with lettuce or spinach leaves.

• **Tuna, Chicken, or Turkey Salad Sandwich**

Prepare one of the recipes from **Multi-Cultural Tuna** (page 59), or **Chicken** (or Turkey) **Chico** (page 56).  Make it into a sandwich with lettuce leaves, tomatoes, and sprouts.

• **Ham Salad Sandwich**

Prepare **I Think Therefore I Ham Salad** (page 57).  Make it into a sandwich with sliced tomatoes or a pineapple ring.

# Tulane Tuna Melt

*That sultry New Orleans heat melts hearts and cheeses alike.*

**2/3**   **bowl** plain tuna fish
   **1**   **soupspoon** mayonnaise (lower cal: hold the mayo)
   **1**   **teaspoon** mustard, Dijon if available
   **1**   **slice** bread, any kind
**Any**   of the following: dash garlic, chopped apple, chopped onion, chopped celery, herbs (such as basil and oregano), Parmesan cheese, sunflower seeds
       Optional toppings: sprouts, tomato slices, cucumber slices
   **1**   **slice** cheese
or **1**   **handful** shredded cheese

Mix the tuna, mayonnaise, mustard, and any of the optional ingredients in a bowl. When everything is blended evenly, flatten the tuna mixture onto the bread. Place any of the optional toppings on the tuna mixture and top with cheese. Place in the microwave, or in the toaster oven on Broil, and watch carefully. Remove just as the cheese starts to melt over the sides of the bread.

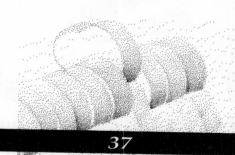

# HAMLET sandwich

**Act I**: *A cafeteria. Enter Cook.*

  **Cook**: *This fare is foul and foul is this fare.*
  **Ham**: *(Aside) A nose by any other name would smell I'm meat.*
  **Cook**: *Zounds! A ham. Let me sandwich it. Where shall I find bread?*
  **Ham**: *Go, get thee to a bunnery.*
  **Bread**: *(Enters) What ho! We are star-crossed loavers.*

**Act II**: *Cook seizes ham slice and thrusts it upon a piece of bread. He rips cheese untimely from salad bar and puts it on top of ham. The Cook placeth the sandwich in the toaster on broil.*

  **Cook**: *Bubble, bubble, broil and trouble,*
  *Toaster burn and cheeses bubble.*

**Act III**: *Cook rubs mustard on a second piece of bread.*

  **Cook**: *Ay, there's the rub.*

**Act IV**: *Cook unites the ham-and-melted-cheese half of the sandwich with the mustard half.*

  **Bread**: *Thus are ham and cheese*
  *'Twixt bread and mustard interpos'd.*
  **Cook**: *To eat or not to eat?*
  *(Cook eats sandwich.)*
  *That is digestion.*

**Act V**: *Ophelia drowns. A festive dance.*

  *Exeunt Omnes.*

*(Recipe follows* 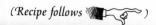 *)*

# HAMLET sandwich

*This sandwich is an enlightened alternative to the cold cold cut sandwich. The recipe also works well with roast beef, corned beef, pastrami, or sliced turkey.*

**2  slices** ham
**2  slices** white, wheat, or rye bread, toasted
**1  slice** cheese, any kind
Mustard and/or mayonnaise **to taste**

Place both ham slices on one piece of toast and top with cheese. Place the bread with ham and cheese in the microwave or in the toaster, on Broil. Keep an eye on it while you are spreading mustard and/or mayonnaise on the other slice of toast. When the cheese has nearly melted, remove from toaster or microwave and top with second slice of toast.

# SCRABBLE Sandwiches

*Make up your own sandwich words, too.*

**P**eanut butter
**J**elly
**H**oney
**B**anana
**G**ranola
**C**ream cheese
**A**pple (sliced thin)
**R**aisins
**Ci**nnamon
**O**range (peeled and sliced in rings)

Take two slices of the bread of your choice and put any combination of any number of these items between them. Use pita bread if you plan to put lots of non-spreadable ingredients (such as raisins or granola) in your sandwich.

Examples: **BACH, COBRA, BOP, GARP, CARP, CiGAR, CARGO, CRAG, JAR, HA**!

# Ripon Reubens

*The cafeteria version of the deli legend, which was invented by Arnold Reuben (1883-1970), an American restaurateur.*

**2** **teaspoons** *Russian Dressing* (page 68, or from the salad bar)
**2** **slices** rye bread, toasted
**2 or 3** **slices** corned beef
**2** **soupspoons** coleslaw or shredded cabbage from the salad bar
**2** **slices** Swiss cheese

Spread Russian dressing on each slice of toast. Place corned beef and then coleslaw on top. Top with cheese. Microwave or broil in toaster oven until cheese melts. Top with remaining slice of toast.

# Pepperdine Pepper Sub

*A colorful way to awaken roast beef.*

**3/4** **bowl** sliced green and/or red peppers
**Enough** steak sauce to cover the peppers
**Enough** roast beef slices for a good-sized sub
**1** sub roll, cut in half lengthwise

Pour the steak sauce over the peppers. Microwave until the sauce is hot, stirring once or twice during cooking. Meanwhile, place the roast beef in the roll. When the pepper sauce is ready, spoon it over the sub. You might need to tackle this one with a knife and fork.

# Cheese Steak

*This recipe is quite good with peppers prepared as in Pepperdine Pepper Sub (page 42).*

| | |
|---|---|
| **Enough** | roast beef **slices** for a good-sized sub |
| **1** | **handful** shredded cheese or several slices cheese |
| **1** | sub roll |
| **Whatever** | you like on your subs: mustard, mayonnaise, lettuce, tomatoes, pickles, onions, hot sauce, etc. |

Put the roast beef on a plate and sprinkle the cheese on top. Microwave until the cheese melts. You may have to rotate the plate for the cheese to melt evenly. Put the cheese-covered roast beef in the sub roll and add your favorite toppings.

# Pocket Full O'Veggies

*A salad sandwich often enjoyed by Cindy Green at Harvard.*

| | |
|---|---|
| **1** | pita bread |
| **1** | salad bar |
| **1** | **handful** shredded cheese |
| or **1** | **soupspoon** salad dressing of your choice (see pages 63-69 to make your own) |

Approach salad bar with empty pita bread. Fill it with the things you'd put in a salad: lettuce, tomato, shredded carrots, chopped turkey, tuna, sprouts, onion slices, etc. Add bacon bits, croutons, sunflower seeds, or something equally crunchy.

Put the cheese in a bowl and melt it in the microwave. Spoon cheese or dressing over the salad inside pita.

# Courtly Cucumber Sandwiches

*"These little gems will turn your cafeteria meal into a garden party," says Eliot Laurence of the School of the Museum of Fine Arts in Boston. Eliot became a cafeteria chef back in high school at the North Carolina School of the Arts.*

Cream cheese
**2 slices** white or wheat bread, toasted
Cucumbers, sliced in thin circles
**1/2 teaspoon** dill (see page 187 to grow your own)

Spread as much cream cheese as you like on both slices of toast. Place 1 or 2 layers of cucumber slices on top of 1 slice of bread. Sprinkle with dill. Top with the other slice of bread. Cut sandwiches into quarters.

# Bard Bagels

*The inventor of this healthy sandwich from Bard College notes that spinach is a good alternative to the often floppy iceberg lettuce and that "the cream cheese will hold it all together."*

Cream cheese
**1** bagel, sliced in half
**2** large spinach leaves
**1 handful** shredded carrots
**1 handful** sliced mushrooms
**1 small handful** sunflower seeds

Spread cream cheese on both bagel halves. On one bagel half, layer on spinach leaves, carrots, mushrooms, and sunflower seeds, and top with other bagel half.

# *Topless Sandwiches*

*Cafeteria chefs under eighteen years of age may not prepare these three sandwiches unless accompanied by parent or guardian.*

• Butter 1 slice of your choice of bread. Top with thin apple slices and sunflower seeds. Add 1 slice cheese. Toast or microwave until the cheese melts.

• Place a few slices of ham, roast beef, or turkey on 1 slice of your favorite bread. Mix 2 soupspoons mustard and 2 soupspoons mayonnaise in a bowl and microwave about 30 seconds, until the mixture is hot. Spoon mustard sauce over meat. Sprinkle with black pepper and eat with knife and fork.

• Spread spicy mustard on your choice of bread. Top with thin layers of: onion, tomato, red or green pepper, and 1 slice cheese. Toast or microwave until the cheese melts.

# *R.I.T B.L.T.*

*Erik Rohde of R.I.T. finds this sandwich—made with breakfast food and lunch food—perfect for brunch.*

| | |
|---:|:---|
| **2** | **slices** white or wheat bread, toasted |
| | Mayonnaise **to taste** |
| **3 or 4** | **strips** bacon |
| **2 or 3** | lettuce leaves |
| **2** | **slices** tomato |

Spread each toast slice with mayonnaise. Pile bacon, lettuce, and tomato on one slice and top with the other slice.

# *Radcliffe Roll-up*

*This recipe, courtesy of Juliet Siler of Harvard, was inspired by a similar sandwich popular in Harvard Square. Use plenty of cheese because, according to Juliet, "Cheese is a big thing at Harvard."*

| | |
|---|---|
| **1** | pita bread (the entire circle) |
| | Mayonnaise and mustard (Dijon, if available) **to taste** |
| **Several** | lettuce leaves |
| **2 or 3** | **slices** turkey |
| **1** | **slice** cheese, Swiss cheese if available |
| **1** | **small handful** shredded carrots |
| **1** | **small handful** sprouts |
| **A few** | **slices** avocado and/or a few rings red onion (optional) |

Lay the pita flat on a plate and spread with mayonnaise and/or mustard. Top with other ingredients, in order, trying to keep them flattened down. Roll up the pita to make a cylinder (secure with a toothpick if necessary). Wrap a napkin around the bottom end and eat from the top down.

# BAT Sandwich (Bacon, Avocado, and Tomato)

|        |              |                  |
|-------:|--------------|------------------|
| 1      | **small handful** | sprouts      |
| 2 or 3 | **strips**   | bacon            |
| 2      | **slices**   | tomato           |
| 2 or 3 | **slices**   | avocado          |
| 1      | **slice**    | bread, toasted   |
| 1      | **soupspoon**| milk             |
| 1/2    | **teaspoon** | mustard          |
| 1/2    | **cup**      | shredded cheese  |

Layer sprouts, bacon, tomato, and avocado on the toast. Add milk and mustard to cheese. Stir and microwave until the cheese melts. Stir again and pour the cheese mixture over the sandwich. You'll probably need to eat this one with a knife and fork.

# PLATO'S PITA POCKET

A STAPLE IN
THE REPUBLIC.

YIELD: ONE
EARTHLY
MANIFESTA-
TION OF THE
FORM OF
SANDWICH.

| | |
|---|---|
| 2 OR 3 | SLICES TOMATO |
| 2 | SOUPSPOONS GREEK FETA CHEESE, CRUMBLED |
| AS MANY | RINGS OF ONION AS YOU LIKE |
| SEVERAL | THIN CUCUMBER SLICES |
| 1 | PITA BREAD |
| 1 | TEASPOON SALAD OIL |
| 1 | TEASPOON VINEGAR |
| DASHES | OF GARLIC POWDER, PARSLEY, AND OREGANO TO TASTE |

STUFF ALL THE VEGETABLES INTO THE PITA. MIX THE OIL, VINEGAR, AND SPICES IN A CUP. DRIZZLE THE DRESSING INTO THE PITA IMMEDIATELY, BEFORE THE OIL AND VINEGAR SEPARATE.

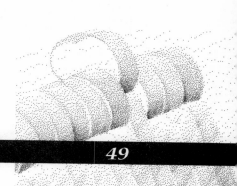

# Lettuce Entertain You

## Creative Salads

Salad bars are getting bigger and more diverse all the time. Many students we spoke to eat salad almost exclusively—different salads for lunch and dinner every day. You'll see that when it comes to salad, lettuce is just the tip of the iceberg.

# Greek Salad

*Pledges who make this salad will make a good impression on their future brothers and sisters. It worked for Neerja Sharma (Delta Gamma) of Boston University.*

**1/2 bowl** lettuce
**3 or 4 chunks** tomato
**1 handful** crumbled feta cheese
**1 small handful** black olives, whole or sliced
*Classic Vinaigrette* dressing (page 65) or oil, vinegar, and black pepper **to taste**

Put all ingredients in bowl with lettuce and toss until blended. Serve with pita bread.

# Carleton Carrot Salad

*Try this crunchy salad on a bed of lettuce or inside pita bread.*

**2 soupspoons** mayonnaise or sour cream (lower cal: substitute plain yogurt)
**2 teaspoons** orange or apple juice
**1 squirt** lemon juice
**1 teaspoon** sugar or honey
**1 almost full bowl** shredded or chopped carrots
**1 small handful** raisins
**1 small handful** granola or sunflower seeds

Mix the mayonnaise, juices, and the sugar in a soup bowl. Stir in the carrots, raisins, and granola until the salad is thoroughly mixed.

# Waldorf Salad

This salad takes its name from the Waldorf-Astoria Hotel in New York City, where, we assume, it was first served. It can be a light lunch served on a bed of lettuce; it's also a nice complement to tuna salad or grilled cheese. Or you can put it inside pita bread or an English muffin with some extra lettuce.

**1 heaping soupspoon** mayonnaise or sour cream (lower cal: substitute plain yogurt)

**A few squirts** lemon juice

**1 teaspoon** sugar or honey

**1** apple, chopped

**1/2 bowl** celery, chopped

**1 small handful** raisins

**1 small handful** granola, nuts, or sunflower seeds

Stir the mayonnaise, lemon juice, and sugar together in a bowl. Toss in the apple, celery, raisins, and granola. Stir thoroughly, until all ingredients are evenly covered by the mayonnaise mixture.

# Cool Cuke Salad

Good in hot weather, or when you wish the weather were hot.

**1/2 bowl** chopped cucumber

**1** orange or 1/2 grapefruit, sectioned, with its juice (see page 61)

**1 heaping soupspoon** sour cream (lower cal: substitute plain yogurt)

**Several squirts** lemon juice

**1/2 teaspoon** mint (see page 187 to grow your own)

Combine all ingredients in a bowl with cucumber. Mix until sour cream and juices are blended thoroughly.

# Basil-Tossed Tomatoes

*Basil and tomatoes were made for each other.*

**1/2** **cup** chopped onions
**1/2** **bowl** chopped tomatoes
**1** **soupspoon** oil, olive oil if available
**1** **soupspoon** vinegar
**1** **soupspoon** grated Parmesan cheese
Salt and pepper **to taste**
**Lots** of basil

Add the onions to the tomatoes. In a cup, blend oil, vinegar, and cheese. Pour dressing over tomatoes and onions immediately, before oil and vinegar separate. Stir to blend thoroughly. Season with salt, pepper, and basil.

# Spinach Salad

*A simple classic.*

**3/4** **bowl** spinach leaves
**1/2** **cup** chopped hard-boiled egg
**1** **soupspoon** bacon bits
**1** **handful** croutons
*Classic Vinaigrette* (page 65) **to taste**

**Several** **dashes** pepper

Cut spinach leaves to a manageable size. Sprinkle egg, bacon bits, and croutons on top. Dress with Classic Vinaigrette (use Italian dressing from the salad bar if you're running late) and season with pepper.

# Festa's Feta Accompli

*Lynn Festa worked in the dining hall during most of her meals at Yale, but looked forward to making this dish on her nights off.*

| | | |
|---:|---|---|
| **1** | **handful** | crumbled feta cheese |
| **1/2** | **bowl** | chopped tomato |
| **1** | **soupspoon** | vinegar |
| **1** | **soupspoon** | oil, olive oil if available |
| **Lots** | | of parsley (see page 187 to grow your own) |

Add the cheese to the tomato. Spoon vinegar and oil on top, and stir until blended. Season with parsley.

## Salads Suited for Sandwiches

See page 36 for sandwich serving ideas. These salads are also good on a bed of lettuce.

# Bill and Ted's Eggcellent Salad

*Most eggregious.*

> 1 **soupspoon** mayonnaise
> 1 **teaspoon** mustard, Dijon mustard if available
> 1 **teaspoon** relish
> 2/3 **bowl** chopped hard-boiled eggs
> Salt and pepper **to taste**
> Bacon bits or chopped black olives (optional)

Add the mayonnaise, mustard, and relish to the eggs and stir until evenly blended. Salt and pepper to taste. Add bacon bits and/or olives.

# Chicken Chico

*Gina Wilson perfected her chicken salad at her high school deli job and later adapted her expert technique to the Chico State cafeteria.*

> 3/4 **bowl** chicken or turkey, chopped into 1/2-inch chunks
> 1 **heaping soupspoon** mayonnaise (lower cal: substitute plain yogurt)
> A few **squirts** lemon juice
> Salt and pepper **to taste**

Blend the mayonnaise thoroughly into the chicken. Add lemon juice and salt and pepper to taste. Then choose one of the two salad styles below.

### • Classic

Stir in:

| | | |
|---|---|---|
| 1/2 | **cup** | chopped celery |
| 1 | **soupspoon** | chopped onions |

### • Artsy

Stir in:

| | | |
|---|---|---|
| 2/3 | **cup** | green grapes, chopped in half crosswise |
| **Lots** | | of tarragon |

# I Think Therefore I Ham Salad

*Not even Descartes could doubt the existence of the perfect ham salad.*

| | | |
|---|---|---|
| 1/2 | **bowl** | chopped ham |
| 1/2 | **cup** | chopped hard-boiled egg |
| 1/2 | **cup** | chopped celery or green pepper |
| 1 | **soupspoon** | mayonnaise |
| 1 | **teaspoon** | mustard |
| **A few** | **squirts** | lemon juice |
| | | Pepper **to taste** |

Combine all ingredients in bowl with ham.  Mix until mayonnaise and mustard are thoroughly blended and egg and celery are distributed evenly.

# Multi-Cultural Tuna

*Expanding the traditional tuna canon.*

Start with:

## • Dead White Male Tuna

**3/4 bowl** plain tuna fish

**1 heaping soupspoon** mayonnaise, if tuna doesn't have mayo on it already (lower cal: substitute plain yogurt)

Spoon the mayonnaise onto the tuna. To diversify, add one of the following groups of ingredients, and stir until thoroughly blended.

## • Asian

**1 teaspoon** soy sauce

**1 small handful** chopped green pepper

**1 small handful** bean sprouts

## • Indian

**1 teaspoon** curry powder

**1 small handful** raisins

**1 small handful** chopped apple

**1 small handful** chopped onion

## • Middle Eastern

*The favorite of Christopher Taylor, Assistant Professor of Religion and Middle East Studies at Drew University.*

**1 small handful** chick peas

**1 small handful** chopped cucumber

**1 heaping teaspoon** *Lemon Vinaigrette* (page 69, or Italian dressing from the salad bar)

## • Continental

**1 teaspoon** mustard, Dijon mustard if available

**1 small handful** chopped celery

**1 small handful** chopped onions

# Orangemen Salad

*Juicy oranges and spicy olives make this salad sweet and sour.*

| | |
|---:|:---|
| **1** | orange, sectioned, with its juice (see next page) |
| **1** | soupspoon chopped onion, red onion if available |
| **4 or 5** | black olives, pitted and sliced |
| **1** | **teaspoon** vinegar |
| **3** | **soupspoons** salad oil |
| **Dash** | garlic powder or garlic salt |
| **Dash** | black pepper |

Mix orange sections, juice, onion, and olive pieces together in a bowl. In a glass, blend vinegar, oil, garlic, and pepper. Pour dressing over oranges and olives right away, before the oil and vinegar separate.

# Frosh Fruit Salad

*Evans Ward designed delightful fruit salads while at the Rhode Island School of Design. His secret: asking the cafeteria staff for any ingredient he wanted if he didn't see it out. "It's who you know," Evans says.*

Take whatever fruits are available, peel them if necessary, and chop them into bite-sized pieces. Section oranges and/or grapefruits according to the method described on the next page. Consider adding shredded coconut, granola, raisins, or even mini marshmallows.

# How to Section an Orange

*Lynn learned this method from the mother in her Mexican exchange family. It's a good trick for fruit salad because you get nice, neat sections and you don't waste the juice.*

**Slice** orange in half as you would a grapefruit (so that individual sections are showing). Pick up one half and **hold** it over a bowl, placing your thumbs where the stem was and your fingertips around the edges of the peel. **Pushing** with your thumbs and **pulling** with your fingers, carefully turn the orange half inside out. The juice will **drain** into the bowl and the sections will **separate** themselves into little triangles that you can now **pull** gently away from the peel. **Remove** any seeds.
**Repeat** process for the other half.
This method also works with grapefruit.

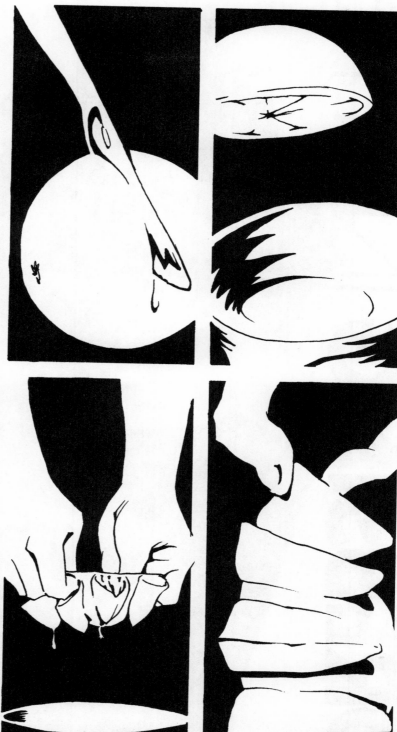

DRESSING IN STYLE

# DRESSING IN STYLE

*TRAY GOURMET's* fashion pages bring you the **hottest dressings** for this season's **coolest salads**

## Make each of these dressings in a beverage glass.

If the trendier ingredients like tarragon vinegar or sesame oil are not available, that's okay—just use whatever you have for now. Then ask the cafeteria supervisor to stock a wider variety.

For all dressings, just put all of the ingredients in a glass and stir. The best way to mix them is to tilt the mixing glass slightly to the side and beat the dressing quickly with a fork, the same way you might beat an egg. The herbs and liquids will stay blended long enough for you to pour the mixture

**Above: Leek in sun-dress. Below: Carrot in flowing coat.**

lovingly on your salad. If you get seconds on salad (these recipes should make enough for two large servings), be sure to stir the dressing again before you reuse it. Don't be afraid to improvise. If the dressing comes out too thin, add a little of the creamy ingredient (such as sour cream); if it's too thick, add a little water or whatever juice the recipe calls for. If it's too sweet, add extra vinegar or lemon juice; if it's too tart, add extra sugar or honey.

If you're calorie counting, substitute plain yogurt for sour cream or mayonnaise, or seek out recipes that call for neither oil nor mayonnaise. It's worth asking cafeteria staff if the yogurt served is low-fat or non-fat, but even regular yogurt has fewer calories per tablespoon than mayonnaise.

Refer to pages 187-191 if you want to grow your own herbs for these dressings.

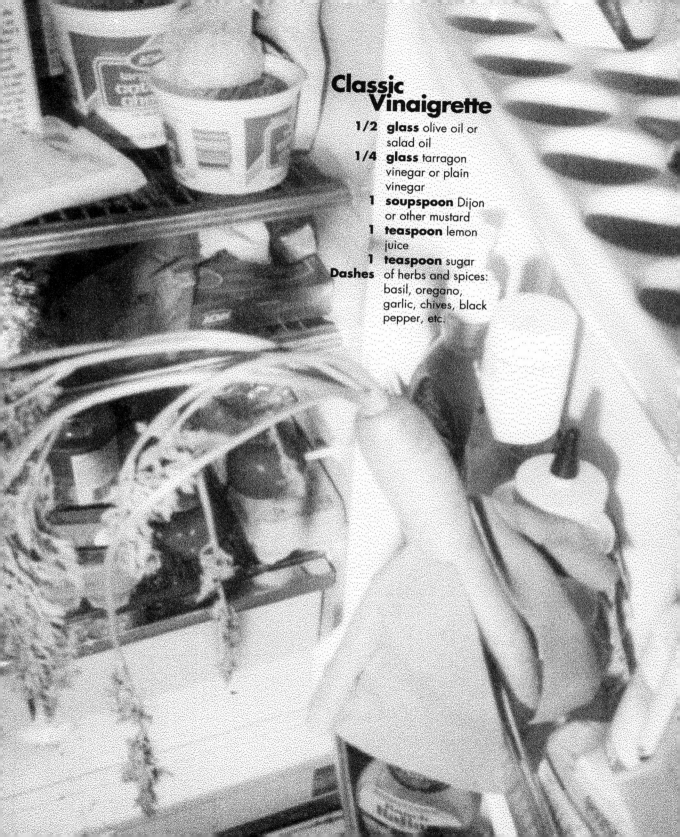

# Classic
# Vinaigrette

**1/2 glass** olive oil or salad oil

**1/4 glass** tarragon vinegar or plain vinegar

**1 soupspoon** Dijon or other mustard

**1 teaspoon** lemon juice

**1 teaspoon** sugar

**Dashes** of herbs and spices: basil, oregano, garlic, chives, black pepper, etc.

# Curry
# DRESSING

- **1/2 glass** sour cream or plain yogurt
- **2 soupspoons** vinegar
- **1 squirt** lemon juice
- **1 teaspoon** honey
- **1 teaspoon** curry powder

## Creamy Italian Dressing

- **1/2 glass** sour cream
- **2 soupspoons** vinegar
- **2 soupspoons** oil
- **1 teaspoon** mustard

Herbs and spices to taste, especially garlic powder, oregano, and red pepper flakes

## Creamy Sesame Dressing

- **1/2 glass** sour cream or plain yogurt
- **2 soupspoons** vinegar
- **1 soupspoon** honey
- **1 soupspoon** sesame oil
- **1 soupspoon** sesame seeds
- **1 soupspoon** soy sauce

# Holy CROSS Dressing

This creamy citrus dressing has graced many a salad prepared by Mary Ann Guillette of Holy Cross.

**1/2 glass** sour cream or plain yogurt
**2 soupspoons** orange juice
**1 soupspoon** lemon juice
**1 teaspoon** honey or sugar

# THOUSAND
## Island Dressing Mix this dressing with chopped
hard-boiled eggs and celery for a great variation on egg salad.

**1/3 glass** mayonnaise

**1 soupspoon** sour cream or plain yogurt

**2 soupspoons** ketchup

**1 heaping soupspoon** relish

**1 teaspoon** Worcestershire sauce, if available

**1 teaspoon** lemon juice

### Russian Dressing

This dressing is a great dip for pieces of raw broccoli and cauliflower—it's the only way to get Lynn to eat them.

**1/3 glass** mayonnaise, sour cream, or plain yogurt

**1/2 cup** ketchup

**1 soupspoon** relish

**Several dashes** black pepper

Juice from one lemon,
**One teaspoon** chopped lemon peel (see Note),
**One teaspoon** honey or sugar,
**One soupspoon** vinegar,
**One-half glass** olive oil or salad oil,
and **Dash** pepper

# Lemon Vinaigrette

**Note:** For the chopped lemon peel: After you squeeze the juice, pull the remaining lemon pulp from one of the quarters. Cut the quarter in half and chop one of the halves into tiny pieces, as small as you have the patience for. The extra lemon flavor is worth the effort.

Choosing SIDES

# Snacks and Side Dishes

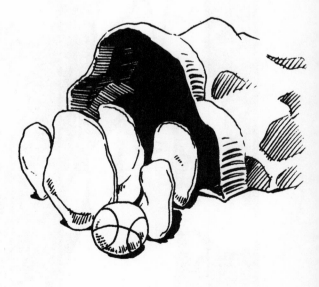

These recipes are good before, during, after (if you're still hungry), and between meals. Or, if you increase the proportions, they can be meals in themselves.

# Nietzsche's Nachos

Let us imagine a coming generation of students with a heroic penchant for the tremendous; let us imagine the bold stride of these dragon slayers, the proud audacity with which they turn their backs on the meagre fare provided them by their cafeteria. Would such as these surrender meekly to the prospect of a plate of dried taco shells or tortilla chips? No! No! A thousand times, no! From such raw stuff they will make a feast — a feast as vital as they themselves, a feast to fuel their dances and their unwavering song. They will cast cheese upon the chips, cheese in every crevice, across every plain and deep in every valley. Then they will bend the cheese to their own unconquerable wills, melting it mercilessly in the microwave. And our new generation will not be without patience! Until the cheese is fully melted will they wait to strew taco sauce like the red promise of dawn across the whole; but this done, and all before them, they will feast as none before.

**1** **plate** of corn chips or broken taco shells
**Many, many** **handfuls** of cheese
**As many** **soupspoons** of hot taco sauce as you dare
Sliced black olives, chopped jalapeño peppers, sour cream **to taste** (optional)

Arrange the chips in more or less one layer so that the cheese and sauce can reach all of them. Heap mounds and mounds of cheese on top, aiming for every chip. Microwave the nachos until the cheese melts. Pour the taco sauce over them, or place in a bowl on the side for dipping. Garnish with olives, peppers, and/or sour cream, if you like.

**Note**: Tufts University trend-spotter Emily Perlman (who has since gone on to American University Film School) notes that you can substitute matzoh for corn chips to make kosher-for-Passover "Machos."

Nietzsche's introduction by Jeff Dolven, Oxford '93.

73

# Potato Nachos

*For when you're in that nacho state of mind, but the cafeteria is in that chipless state of being.*

**1**   baked potato, sliced thinly
**1**   **cup** taco sauce
**1 or 2**   **handfuls** shredded cheese
    Sliced black olives, chopped jalapeño peppers, sour cream **to taste** (optional)

Arrange potato slices in one layer on a plate. Cover with taco sauce. Sprinkle cheese and any other garnishes on top. Microwave until the cheese melts.

# Pita Drizzles

*A crispy, spicy, unusual complement to any meal.*

**1**   pita bread
**2**   **pats** butter (lower cal: skip the butter)
    Tabasco sauce **to taste**
    Soy sauce **to taste**

Split the pita around the circumference to form two circles. Spread one pat of butter on each circle. Drizzle tabasco sauce over the pita in horizontal stripes. Then drizzle soy sauce over the pita in vertical stripes. (You are, of course, welcome to come up with your own design.) Toast until crispy.

# Greased Lightning Garlic Bread

*Delicious but not recommended for important dates.*

**As many** **slices** of bread as you want
**Lots** of butter
Garlic salt or garlic powder **to taste**
Chopped parsley

If you use a toaster oven, spread each bread slice with butter, sprinkle with garlic and parsley, and toast until butter melts and edges are golden brown. For French bread, slice the loaf lengthwise, spread the butter, garlic, and parsley on each half, and toast.

If you use a microwave, put the butter, garlic, and parsley in a bowl and microwave until the butter melts. Meanwhile, toast your bread. Stir the melted butter and drizzle on the toast.

## •Greased Lightning Garlic Bread with Cheese

Follow recipe for Greased Lightning Garlic Bread. If you use a toaster oven, put a handful of cheese on top of the butter and herbs before you toast the bread. If you use a microwave, melt a handful of cheese in a bowl after you melt the butter. Spoon melted cheese over the toast after you spread the butter.

# *Pa amb Tomaquet* (Bread with Tomato)

*Lynn spent the summer before sophomore year in Barcelona and came back an expert with this Catalan specialty (see also Espinacs amb Panses i Pinyons, page 83).*

**6-inch length** French bread (French is best, but you can use any kind)
**Several** tomato **wedges**
Olive oil **to taste**
Salt and pepper **to taste**

Slice French bread in half lengthwise. Rub the tomato wedges, cut side down, on the bread so that it turns light red. Drizzle a few spoonfuls of olive oil over the bread, add a few dashes of salt and pepper, and microwave or toast until hot.

# *Parmesan Toast*

*Larry's roommate Andrew Michaelson picked this one up from his father. How much Parmesan cheese should you use? "Enough so that you can smell it across the state line," says Andrew.*

**1 slice** bread
Grated Parmesan cheese

Cover bread with Parmesan cheese. Toast until cheese is warm and softened.

# Pesto Muffins

Pesto is an Italian sauce made with green herbs, usually basil. It is so delicious that you might want to consider planting a double patch of basil in your herb garden (see page 187). Pesto fans should also try Pesto Pasta, page 94.

1 **soupspoon** grated Parmesan cheese
2 **soupspoons** chopped basil leaves
**Dash** garlic powder or garlic salt
2 **teaspoons** oil, olive oil if available
1 English muffin, split

Combine cheese, basil, and garlic in a cup. While stirring, slowly add the oil. Blend thoroughly. If you are using dried basil, give it some time to soak up the oil. Spread half of the pesto mixture on each muffin half, and toast or microwave until warm.

# Blue Devil Eggs

A dish fit for a duke. Eat them by themselves or use them to garnish a salad.

2 hard-boiled eggs
1 **teaspoon** mayonnaise
1/2 **teaspoon** mustard
1/2 **teaspoon** relish
Paprika, if available, and/or parsley

Slice the eggs lengthwise. Scoop out the yolk halves and put them in a bowl. Put the whites aside.
Add the mayonnaise, mustard, and relish to the yolks and mash with a fork until creamy. Place a spoonful of yolk mixture back into each of the empty white halves. Sprinkle a bit of paprika and/or parsley on top.

# Tarheel Taters

*Any of these four options can be a meal in itself.*

Slice a hot baked potato lengthwise, cutting about 2/3 of the way through to the bottom. Stuff with one of the following fillings.

• Fill potato with raw or cooked broccoli, top with a handful of cheese, and microwave until the cheese melts. Season with black pepper.

• Spoon in a few soupspoons of sour cream and top with bacon bits, croutons, and chives.

• In a bowl, combine 1/2 bowl chopped mushrooms, 2 soupspoons chopped onions, 2 soupspoons soy sauce, and 2 pats butter. Microwave until the butter melts, stir until well blended, and spoon into potato while still hot.

• Fill potato with 1 soupspoon each chopped onions and chopped green peppers. Add 3 soupspoons taco sauce, and top with 1 handful cheese. Microwave until cheese melts.

# Fond O' You Cheese Fondue

*Our most famous, most requested, most imitated recipe. It's great for entertaining large groups of friends in the cafeteria—in which case you'll need to make several bowls.*

| | | |
|---|---|---|
| **2/3** | **bowl** | cheese, grated or chopped (use several kinds of cheese, if available) |
| **2** | **soupspoons** | grated Parmesan cheese |
| **3** | **pats** | butter |
| **1** | **soupspoon** | mustard |
| **3** | **soupspoons** | cream or sour cream |
| **A few** | **dashes** | garlic powder, oregano, basil, or nutmeg |
| | | Food for dipping (see the following) |

Combine all ingredients in a bowl with the cheese. Microwave until the cheese is thoroughly melted. Stir until smooth and creamy.

Food for dipping, stuck on the end of a fork:

- **Bread squares** — French bread is best, but any kind is fine.

- **Steak, chicken, hamburger** — Remove from bone, if necessary, and cut into bite-sized pieces.

- **Apples, pears** — Cut into eighths.

- **Any vegetables** — Try carrot and celery sticks or cherry tomatoes.

- **Crackers** — Any kind.

# Holy Guacamole!

*A Mexican avocado dip that has made its way north into trendy restaurants and college cafeterias.*

| | | |
|---|---|---|
| **2/3** | **bowl** | avocado chunks |
| **1** | **teaspoon** | mayonnaise, sour cream, or plain yogurt |
| **1** | **soupspoon** | Mexican salsa, if available |
| **A few** | **squirts** | lemon juice |
| **A few** | **drops** | Tabasco sauce |
| **A few** | **dashes** | garlic powder or garlic salt |
| | Salt | **to taste** |

Mash the avocado chunks with a fork. Add other ingredients and keep mashing with the fork until everything is blended. Eat with taco chips or good bread.

# Three Delicious Dips

*Serve with crackers or veggies such as carrots, celery, cucumbers, green peppers, etc. They feed more than one—pass them around.*

## • *Spicy Orange Dip* (low-cal)

| | | |
|---|---|---|
| **1** | **cup** | plain yogurt |
| **2** | **soupspoons** | orange juice |
| **1/2** | **teaspoon** | chili powder |

Combine all ingredients in a bowl. Be sure the chili powder is thoroughly blended.

### • Nutty Feta Dip

|  |  |  |
|---|---|---|
| **1** | **cup** | crumbled feta cheese |
| **2** | **soupspoons** | oil, olive if available |
| **1** | **soupspoon** | cream or milk |
| **1/2** | **cup** | chopped nuts or chopped sunflower seeds |
| **Dash** | | black pepper |

Put feta, oil, and cream in a bowl and mash with a fork.  The mixture should be creamy and blended thoroughly.  Sprinkle the nuts and pepper on top.

### • Herb Dip

|  |  |  |
|---|---|---|
| **3/4** | **cup** | cottage cheese |
| **3/4** | **cup** | sour cream |
| **A lot** | | of herbs, preferably ones you've grown in your own garden (see page 187), including oregano, dill, basil, chives, etc. |
| **A few** | **squirts** | lemon juice |

Put all ingredients in a bowl and blend thoroughly with a fork.

# Celery Snacks

*Bound to bring back fond memories of your lunchbox.*

| | |
|---|---|
| **Several** | celery stalks (unsliced, if possible, so that they're still in a "U" shape) |
| | Peanut butter |
| | Raisins (optional) |

Spread celery stalks with peanut butter.  Top with raisins.

## Vegetable Dishes

Here are some creative ways to improve upon dull cafeteria vegetables. Use these recipes and you won't miss out on that valuable source of nutrition.

# Cauliflower Vinaigrette

*Caulilfower has been cultivated since Roman times. Plain cafeteria cauliflower may taste like it was cultivated in Roman times. Here is a way to renew its flavor.*

1 **teaspoon** mustard, Dijon if available
1 **teaspoon** chopped parsley or oregano
1 **soupspoon** vinegar
3 **soupspoons** oil, olive if available
1 **serving** cooked cauliflower
Grated Parmesan cheese **to taste**

Combine mustard, herbs, vinegar, and oil in a glass. Pour the dressing over the cauliflower. Warm up in microwave, if you like. Season with Parmesan cheese.

# Honey Glazed Carrots

*Sweet and crunchy.*

1 **handful** granola
1 **soupspoon** honey
2 **pats** butter
1 **serving** cooked carrots from the serving line

Sprinkle granola over carrots. Put honey and butter together in a cup. Microwave until the butter melts. Stir well and pour over carrots. Reheat carrots briefly if they've gotten cold.

# Kenyon Korn

*Anne Seiler of Kenyon, the author of this recipe, does know how to spell "corn."*

**3** **soupspoons** corn (from either the food line or the salad bar)
**1** **handful** chopped green peppers
**1** **handful** chopped onion
**2** **teaspoons** mustard
**1** **serving** rice
**1** **handful** shredded cheese

Put the corn, peppers, onion, and mustard on top of the rice and stir until the mustard is thoroughly blended. Sprinkle the cheese on top, but do not stir it in. Microwave until the cheese melts.

# Espinacs amb Panses i Pinyons

(Spinach with Raisins and Pine Nuts)

*A Catalan specialty that Lynn imported from Barcelona. Pronounce the title any way you want to. Try it with Pa Amb Tomaquet (page 76).*

**1** **soupspoon** oil, olive if available
**1** **handful** raisins
**1** **handful** sunflower seeds (or pine nuts, if available)
**2** **soupspoons** chopped ham (optional)
**1** **serving** cooked spinach

Distribute ingredients evenly on top of spinach, stir, and microwave until hot. Stir again.

# Creamed Spinach

*Somehow, any vegetable tastes good when you heap it with cream and cheese.*

**1 soupspoon** cream, half-and-half, or milk
**1 serving** cooked spinach
**1 handful** shredded cheese
**Several dashes** pepper

Stir the cream into the spinach. Top with cheese. Microwave until the cheese melts. Stir the melted cheese into the spinach. Season with pepper.

# Buckeye Brussels Sprouts

*If you are concerned about this cookbook's slight anti-Brussels sprout bias, see "Improvising and Substituting," page 11.*

**3 pats** butter
**1 teaspoon** sugar
**1 serving** cooked Brussels sprouts

Put the butter and sugar in a cup and microwave until butter melts. Stir until sugar dissolves. Pour glaze over Brussels sprouts.

# Broccoli with Lemon Butter

*Even George Bush would like this one.*

**5**   **pats** butter
     Juice of half a lemon
**1**   **serving** cooked broccoli
**Dash**   pepper

Put the butter and lemon juice in a cup and microwave until the butter melts. Stir and pour over broccoli. Season with pepper.

# Tomatoes Provençal

*This dish is usually made by stuffing whole tomatoes, but we just turn the recipe inside out.*

**3/4**   **cup** croutons (crush them in a bowl using the bottom of a glass)
**1**   **teaspoon** onions, chopped small
**4**   **pats** butter
**Several**   tomato **wedges or slices**
**A few**   **dashes** basil or oregano

Put the croutons, onions, and butter in a bowl. Microwave until the butter melts and then stir until blended. Spoon mixture over tomato wedges. Sprinkle with basil or oregano. Microwave until tomatoes are warm.

# Green Beans in Peanut Sauce

*The cafeteria adaptation of the Chinese restaurant favorite.*

**1  soupspoon** peanut butter, crunchy if available
**1  teaspoon** soy sauce
**1/2  teaspoon** sugar
**Dash**  garlic powder or garlic salt
**1  serving** cooked green beans

Put the peanut butter, soy sauce, sugar, and garlic in a cup.  Microwave until peanut butter softens.  Stir until thoroughly blended.  Add a little hot water if it is hard to mix.  Pour mixture over green beans and stir until they are coated.

# Green Beans Almondine with Mushrooms

*While visiting Yale, Julia Child remarked, "The loneliest thing I've ever seen is a frozen string bean." Here is a way to keep it company.*

**1  small handful** sliced almonds (Sliced almonds may be found at the baked potato bar or the sundae bar; otherwise, use sunflower seeds, granola, or another type of nut)
**1  small handful** sliced mushrooms
**3  pats** butter
**1  serving** cooked green beans
Salt and pepper **to taste**

Put the almonds and mushrooms in a bowl with the butter.  Microwave until the butter melts. Stir.  Pour the mixture over the beans while still hot.  Season with salt and pepper.

# Potatoes au Gratin

*You can use the mashed potatoes as served, or you can scoop the insides out of a baked potato and mash them with a fork.*

**1 soupspoon** milk or cream
**1 serving** mashed potatoes or 1 baked potato
**1 pat** butter
**2 soupspoons** grated Parmesan cheese or 1 handful shredded cheese
Chopped parsley
Salt and pepper **to taste**

Pour the milk or cream over the potatoes and mix slightly. Place the butter pat on top and sprinkle with cheese. Microwave until the butter and cheese melt and then stir to blend thoroughly. Season with parsley, salt, and pepper.

# Zukes with Herbs

*Heather Pearl Cromie went west to San Francisco State University and discovered this mellow way to prepare zucchini (To grow your own herbs, see pages 187-191).*

**1 serving** zucchini, cooked or raw
**2 pats** butter
**Lots** of herbs: parsley, chives, dill, tarragon, basil, etc.
**1/2 cup** crushed croutons (crush them in a bowl using the bottom of a glass)

Top zucchini with butter while zucchini is still hot. Sprinkle herbs on top while the butter is melting, and then top with crushed croutons. Microwave to melt butter if zucchini gets cold.

MAIN DISHES

# REBEL WITHOUT A SAUCE

## Rehabilitating Plain Pasta

*You can rebel against boring cafeteria pasta. First, prepare one of our special sauces. Then ask for pasta without the sauce on the serving line—this way the pasta will still be hot when you add your sauce.*

*Rice works just as well as pasta in these recipes.*

# Pasta with
# EAT THE SYSTEM
# S·A·U·C·E·S

Some of the best pasta recipes can be made with our collection of Eat the System sauces (see page 147). Prepare the sauce of your choice and pour it over plain pasta.

Our favorites are:

**Pasta with Claudio's Salsa di Pomodoro** (page 148)

**Pasta with Mushroom Sauce** (page 149)

**Pasta with Garlic Butter** (page 151)

# Favorite Fettucine Alfredo

*One of our most popular recipes.*

**2** **heaping soupspoons** sour cream (lower cal: substitute plain yogurt)
**1** **big handful** shredded cheese or 2 slices of cheese
**3** **soupspoons** grated Parmesan cheese
**2** **pats** butter (lower cal: skip the butter)
**1** **soupspoon** cream or milk
**Lots** of grated Parmesan cheese
Pepper **to taste**
**1** **serving** plain pasta

Combine everything except the pasta in a bowl. Microwave until the butter and cheese are completely melted. Stir until smooth, adding extra cream or milk if mixture is stiff.

Pour the sauce over the pasta. Sprinkle some more Parmesan cheese on top, if you like.

# Aglio e Olio (Italian garlic and oil pasta)

*The best part is soaking up the remaining garlicky oil with a piece of bread.*

**Several** **dashes** garlic powder or garlic salt
**1/2** **cup** oil, olive oil if available
**1** **serving** plain pasta
Salt and pepper **to taste**
Grated Parmesan cheese **to taste**

Add the garlic to the oil and microwave until oil is hot. Pour over pasta and toss until blended. Season with salt and pepper and sprinkle with grated Parmesan cheese.

# Chinese Peanut Pasta

*A standard in Chinese restaurants, where it is often called Sesame Noodles.*

**3 soupspoons** peanut butter, crunchy if available
**2 soupspoons** soy sauce
**1 soupspoon** sugar
**1 soupspoon** oil, sesame oil if available
**1 serving** plain pasta
**Several** cucumber **slices**, cut into slivers (optional)

Place all ingredients except the pasta and cucumbers in a bowl. Microwave until the peanut butter is soft enough to mix into the other liquids. Stir mixture until smooth. Pour it over the pasta and stir until the noodles are evenly covered. Some like it hot; some like to let it cool to room temperature before eating. Garnish with cucumbers, if you like.

# Pesto Pasta

*If you grow only one herb yourself (see pages 187-191), grow basil, just so you can make this dish.*

**2 heaping soupspoons** chopped basil
**1 soupspoon** grated Parmesan cheese
**Dash** garlic powder or garlic salt
**2 soupspoons** oil, olive oil if available, or 8 pats butter, melted in the microwave
**1 serving** plain pasta
Salt and pepper **to taste**

Mix basil, cheese, and garlic together in a bowl. Add oil or melted butter slowly, while stirring. Heat mixture in the microwave until oil is hot. Pour over pasta and toss until well blended. Season with salt and pepper.

# Pasta Primavera

*This recipe is as colorful as primavera (spring, that is).*

**2/3** **cup** raw or cooked broccoli, chopped
**1** **handful** chopped onions
**1** **handful** chopped green peppers and/or celery
**1** **handful** chopped tomatoes
**3** **soupspoons** soy sauce
**1** **soupspoon** orange juice
**1** **pat** butter
**1** **serving** plain pasta
**1** **handful** shredded cheese

Put all vegetables in a bowl and pour the soy sauce and orange juice over them. Top with butter and shredded cheese and microwave until the butter and cheese melt. Stir, pour over pasta, and stir again.

# History of Artichoke Pasta

*Yale art history major Harriet Fennell wishes this dish could have counted for her final project.*

**3/4** **cup** chopped artichoke hearts (cut in squares for cubist effect)
**1** **soupspoon** oil, olive oil if available
**1** **teaspoon** basil
**1/2** **cup** sour cream or yogurt
**1** **serving** plain pasta
Pepper and grated Parmesan cheese **to taste**

Put artichoke hearts, oil, and basil in a bowl. Microwave until oil is hot. Add sour cream and stir until blended. Pour over pasta and toss. Arrange impressionistically on plate. Season with pepper and grated cheese, demonstrating pointillistic influence.

# Pepper Pasta

*Consider adding hot pimentos or chili peppers, if available.*

**2 soupspoons** oil
**1 soupspoon** Worcestershire sauce
**3/4 bowl** red and/or green peppers, sliced in thin strips
**Dash** garlic powder or garlic salt
**1 serving** plain pasta
**Dash** black pepper

Pour oil and Worcestershire sauce over peppers in bowl. Add garlic and microwave until oil is hot. Stir, pour over pasta, and stir again. Season with pepper.

# Algerian Pasta

*Invented by Jon Alger of Yale, who points out that it is "a delightful mix of textures and surprising flavors, and it's colorful, too."*

**2 soupspoons** tuna
**1 handful** raw broccoli
**1 handful** chopped red peppers
**1 serving** plain pasta
**Several pats** butter, cut into small pieces

Arrange tuna and broccoli and red peppers over pasta. Place butter pieces on top. Microwave until the butter melts and stir until blended.

# Pasta with Oregano Cream

A former restaurant writer at the Yale Daily News, Larry's roommate Jay Withgott (now at the University of Arkansas) adapted this recipe from one of his favorite New Haven restaurants.

**1/2** **cup** cream

**2** **pats** butter

**1** **soupspoon** oregano

**Dash** salt and pepper

**1/2** **bowl** chopped vegetables of your choice (tomatoes, broccoli, peppers, etc.)

**1** **serving** plain pasta

Combine the cream, butter, and spices with vegetables. Microwave until mixture is warm. Pour over pasta and blend well.

**WEAK WORLD NEWS**

August 16, 1992    75¢/80¢ CANADA    182596

JFK's Frozen Psychic PREDICTS chilling cafeteria breakthrough!

# COLLEGE SLEUTHS SOLVE THE MYSTERY MEAT AFTER A VISIT FROM ELVIS...FROM BEYOND THE GRAVY!

**Let's Face It, He Knew an Awful Lot About Food!**

**EXCLUSIVE!**

# SOLVING THE MYSTERY MEAT

**Beef or Hamburger with**

# EAT THE SYSTEM
## S·A·U·C·E·S

*Our Eat the System sauces (pages 147-151) can do a lot for plain beef and burgers. Prepare your choice of sauce, spread over a serving of meat, and microwave until hot.*

We recommend:

***Beef or Burger with Barbecue Sauce*** (page 149)
***Beef or Burger with Mustard Sauce*** (page 150)
***Beef or Burger with Mushroom Sauce*** (page 149)
***Beef or Burger with Sweet and Sour Sauce***
    (page 150)
***Steak with Teriyaki Sauce*** (page 151)

BEEF
Recipes

# Bistec Moutarde et Champignons

(Steak with mustard and mushrooms)

*This topping will make dry roast beef juicier and tastier. You can also substitute a hamburger for the roast beef and eat it on a bun or on slices of toasted rye bread.*

| | | |
|---|---|---|
| **1** | **handful** | chopped mushrooms |
| **4** | **pats** | butter |
| **2** | **soupspoons** | cream |
| **1** | **soupspoon** | mustard |
| **Dash** | | thyme |
| **Dash** | | garlic powder or garlic salt |
| **1** | **serving** | roast beef or 1 hamburger |

Put all ingredients except the beef into a bowl and microwave them until the butter melts. Stir until the mushrooms are covered evenly. Pour the mixture over the beef and spread it out evenly.

# Beef Enchiladas

*Do not despair if there are no tortillas in the cafeteria. Just make pita tortillas — cut a piece of pita bread around the edges to make two circles.*

| | | |
|---|---|---|
| **3/4** | **bowl** | roast beef or hamburger, chopped |
| **Lots** | | of taco sauce |
| **2** | | tortillas or 1 pita pocket cut into 2 pita tortillas |
| **Several** | **handfuls** | shredded cheese |
| | | Chopped black olives (optional) |

Pile meat and a few spoonfuls of taco sauce in the center of each tortilla. Roll each one up (secure with toothpick if necessary). Pour more sauce on top, add cheese, and top with black olives, if you like. Microwave until cheese melts. Serve with extra taco sauce.

# Burger Heaven

*Seems like they always serve hamburgers, doesn't it? But they don't always have to taste the same. Prepare these toppings to go between the burger and the bun.*

### • Greek Week Burger

**2 or 3**   tomato slices
**2  soupspoons** feta cheese
**1  soupspoon** chopped pimento peppers

Top burger with tomato slices, feta, and then peppers.

### • Michigan Go Bleu Burger

**1  soupspoon** bleu cheese dressing
**1  handful** sprouts
**A few  rings** onion

Pour dressing on top of burger and top with sprouts and onions.

### • Todd's Taco Burger

**1  handful** cheese
**2  soupspoons** taco sauce
**A few**  lettuce leaves
**1  handful** sprouts and/or shredded carrots (optional)

*By adding carrots and sprouts, Todd Crowell of the University of Montana rescues this burger from the realm of junk food.*

Top burger with cheese and then taco sauce. Microwave bunless burger until cheese melts. Put on bottom bun, add lettuce, sprouts and/or carrots, and replace top bun.

### • Bitchin' Surf Burger

**1** **slice** cheese, Swiss cheese if available
**2 or 3** tomato **slices**
**2 or 3** avocado **slices**

Put cheese on burger and microwave it without a bun until the cheese melts. Place on bun and top with tomato, avocado, and other bun half.

### • Mushroom Burger

**1** **soupspoon** chopped onions
**2** **soupspoons** steak sauce
**1/2** **cup** chopped mushrooms

Add onions and steak sauce to mushrooms. Microwave until hot and stir well. Put on top of hamburger and replace other bun half.

### • Reuben Burger

**1** **slice** Swiss cheese
**1** **soupspoon** Russian dressing
**2** **soupspoons** cole slaw or shredded cabbage from the salad bar

Top burger with cheese. Microwave bunless burger until cheese melts. Place on bun and top with dressing, coleslaw, and other bun half.

### • Bacon Burger

**2 or 3** **strips** bacon
**1** **slice** Swiss or Cheddar cheese

Top burger with bacon, then cheese. Microwave bunless burger until cheese starts to melt. Put on bun and add other bun half.

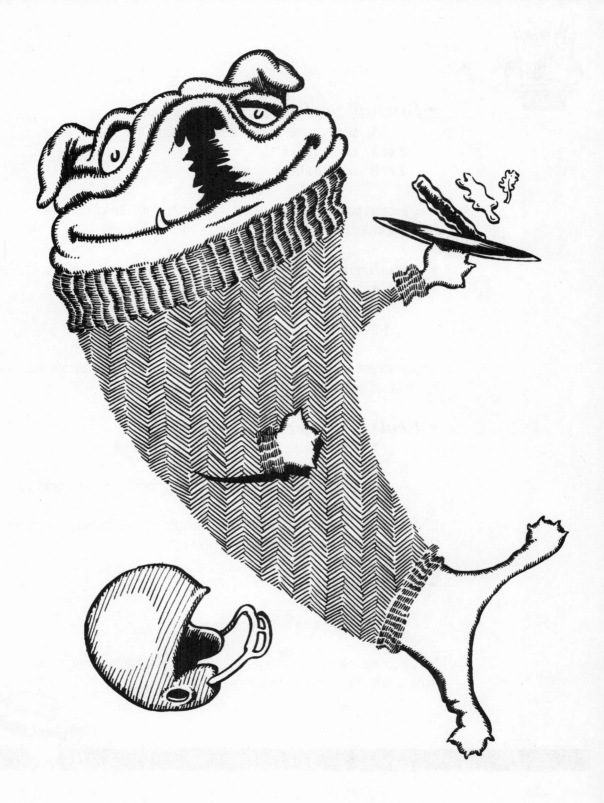

# BULLDOG BEEF

*Enjoyed from New Haven to Atlanta, a beef dish with bite.*

| | | |
|---:|:---|:---|
| 2 | **soupspoons** | Worcestershire sauce |
| 1 | **teaspoon** | lemon juice |
| A few | **drops** | Tabasco sauce |
| Lots | of black pepper | |
| 1 | **serving** | roast beef or 1 hamburger |
| | Chopped parsley and/or chives | |

Combine the Worcestershire sauce, lemon juice, Tabasco sauce, and black pepper in a bowl and microwave until hot.  Stir again and pour over roast beef.  Microwave briefly to warm up, if you like.  Season with more pepper and some parsley or chives.

# Beef Stroganoff

*This dish is tasty served on top of rice, noodles, or even potatoes.*

**1/2 cup** chopped onions
**1/2 cup** chopped mushrooms
**3 pats** butter
**1/2 cup** gravy (from the serving line)
**1 soupspoon** ketchup
**1 soupspoon** sour cream
**1 teaspoon** mustard
**1 serving** roast beef or 1 hamburger, chopped
**1 serving** rice, plain pasta, or potatoes

Put onions and mushrooms together in bowl, add butter, and microwave until butter melts. Meanwhile, combine gravy, ketchup, sour cream, and mustard in another bowl. Add buttered mushrooms and onions and blend together. Add meat to mixture. Microwave all together to warm them up. Pour over rice, pasta, or potatoes.

# Beef with Peanut Sauce

*This easy and exotic recipe was invented by an easy and exotic Yale alum.*

**3 soupspoons** peanut butter
**1 soupspoon** Worcestershire sauce
**1 soupspoon** lemon juice
**1 soupspoon** sugar, brown sugar, or honey
**1 soupspoon** soy sauce
**Dash** ginger, if available
**1 serving** roast beef or 1 hamburger, chopped

Combine all ingredients except beef in a bowl and microwave until peanut butter is soft enough to stir. Stir until blended and pour over beef.

## Pork Recipes

# Pork à l'Orange

*Meat and fruit is a trendy combination, but* Tray Gourmet*'s fashion consultants say this one will never go out of style.*

**1** orange
**2 pats** butter
**3 soupspoons** orange juice
**1 teaspoon** vinegar
**1 teaspoon** honey
**2** pork chops or pork slices

Cut the orange in half. Section one half of the orange in a bowl (see page 61 for how to section an orange). Set the other half of the orange aside. Put butter, orange juice, vinegar, and honey in bowl with sectioned orange. Microwave until butter melts, stir, and microwave again until hot. Spoon onto pork and microwave again to warm it up if you like. Garnish with rings of orange cut from the unused orange half.

# PeRiOdIc Table Pork

*This spicy recipe is hot enough to blow up the chem lab.*

**1/2 bowl** ketchup
**1 soupspoon** lemon juice
**Dash** cinnamon
**Several dashes** red pepper flakes
**As many drops** Tabasco sauce as you dare
**1 serving** pork

Mix all ingredients except pork in bowl with ketchup. Microwave until hot. Spread on pork. Serve with a pitcher of $H_2O$.

**EAT THE SYSTEM**

S·A·U·C·E·S

Our Eat the System Sauces perk up plain pork. Prepare your choice of sauce, spread over a serving of pork, and microwave until hot.

Definitely try:

**Pork with Barbecue Sauce** (page 149)

**Pork with Mustard Sauce** (page 150)

**Pork with Sweet and Sour Sauce** (page 150)

PORK

Recipes

# *Application Apple Chops*

*Remember how good it felt to get all of your college applications in? That's how good this recipe will taste.*

**1** apple, cored and thinly sliced
**2** **pats** butter
**1** **teaspoon** vinegar
**2** **soupspoons** apple juice
**1** **teaspoon** sugar
**2** pork chops or pork slices

Put apple slices in bowl and add butter, vinegar, juice, and sugar. Microwave until the butter melts and stir well. Continue to microwave until mixture is thoroughly hot. Spoon mixture on top of pork and microwave again to warm it up if you like.

EAT THE SYSTEM
S·A·U·C·E·S

*Our Eat the System Sauces (page 147) work wonders with plain ham.  Prepare your choice of sauce, spread over a serving of ham, and microwave until hot.*

You should sample:

**Ham with Barbecue Sauce** (page 149)
**Ham with Mushroom Sauce** (page 149)
**Ham with Mustard Sauce** (page 150)

# Holden Caulfield's "Crumby" Ham

*Those crushed croutons, you think they're bread crumbs, but if you ask me, they're just phonies, all of 'em.*

**2/3** **cup** crushed croutons (crush in a bowl with the bottom of a glass)
Juice of a few lemon wedges
**2** **pats** butter
**1/2** **teaspoon** honey
**1** **serving** ham

Put the croutons in a bowl with the lemon juice, butter, and honey. Microwave until the butter melts. Stir to distribute the melted butter. Spoon crumb topping over ham and microwave again briefly to warm it up. Add extra lemon juice if you like.

# Menlo Melon

*California colleges get a longer melon season for this recipe.*

**2** cantaloupe wedges
**3 or 4** ham **slices**
Toothpicks

Cut the cantaloupe into 1-inch chunks by first slicing the whole wedge off the rind and then slicing the wedge into pieces crosswise. Slice the ham into 1-inch-wide strips until you have one ham strip for each melon chunk. Wrap one ham strip around each melon chunk and secure with toothpick.

# Hoosier Ham

*The cafeteria twist on the classic style of serving ham with fruit.*

**1/2 cup** apple juice
**1 soupspoon** vinegar
**2 dashes** cinnamon
**1 small handful** raisins
**1/3 bowl** grape jelly

Add juice, vinegar, cinnamon, and raisins to grape jelly and microwave until hot. Stir well and pour over ham. Heat up again in the microwave, if you like.

# Delicious Cafeteria Meatloaf Recipes*

*Years of research have yielded no results in this area.

# CHICKENING OUT

If your cafeteria doesn't get much more innovative with chicken than "baked," "broiled," or "with brown sauce on the side" then you have the perfect chicken to prepare these recipes with.
First prepare the sauce or topping, then get the chicken hot from the serving line.

**Note**: These recipes work with turkey, too.

*Eat the System Sauces (pages 147-151) definitely change chicken for the better. Prepare your choice of sauce, spread over a serving of chicken, and microwave until hot.*

Some of our favorites are:

**Chicken with Claudio's Salsa di Pomodoro**
(page 148)
**Chicken with Barbecue Sauce** (page 149)
**Chicken with Sweet and Sour Sauce** (page 150)
**Chicken with Teriyaki Sauce** (page 151)

# California Chicks

Courtesy of Kirsten Evans of University of California at Santa Cruz. Kirsten and Lynn played together all the time when they were little. The closest they ever got to cooking together, though, was mixing chocolate milk and pickle juice together and talking Kirsten's little brother Derek into drinking it.

**6** **pats** butter
**2/3** **bowl** sliced mushrooms
**1 or 2** **pieces** baked or broiled chicken
**1** **handful** cheese
Salt and pepper **to taste**

Add the butter to the mushrooms. Microwave until the butter melts, stir, and pour over the chicken. Top with cheese. Microwave again until the cheese starts to melt.

# "Great Chicken, Honey"

Your dining-hall date will compliment you by repeating this dish's title (For more dirt on dining-hall dating, see page 174).

**2** **soupspoons** honey
**2** **soupspoons** lemon juice
**2** **pieces** plain baked or broiled chicken, with or without skin
**2/3** **cup** crushed croutons (crush them in a bowl with the bottom of a glass)

Stir the honey and lemon juice together in a cup until smooth. Spread the mixture over the chicken with a knife. Sprinkle the crushed croutons over the now-sticky chicken. Warm up in the microwave, if you like.

# Chinese Chicken with Cashews

*Why pay for takeout and delivery when you can create this Chinese restaurant favorite in the cafeteria?*

**1 or 2**   **pieces** baked or broiled chicken
**3**   **soupspoons** soy sauce
**1**   **soupspoon** oil, sesame oil or peanut oil if available
**1**   **teaspoon** sugar
**Dash**   ginger
**Dash**   garlic powder or garlic salt
**1**   **handful** cashews, peanuts, walnuts, or sunflower seeds

The authentic way: Remove the skin from the chicken. Cut the meat off of the bones and into 1/2-inch cubes.
The easy way: Remove the skin from the chicken, but leave the meat on the bone. Once chicken is prepared, combine all ingredients except chicken in a bowl and microwave until hot. Stir until the sugar is dissolved. Pour the mixture over the chicken immediately.

# Chicken Pekel

*We named this recipe after Kent Pekel to show him that we're thinking of him while he's teaching in China, where he named his students after his friends from Yale.*

| | | |
|---:|---|---|
| **2** | **soupspoons** | salad oil |
| **1** | **soupspoon** | vinegar |
| **3** | **soupspoons** | grated Parmesan cheese |
| **1** | **teaspoon** | mustard |
| **2** | **pieces** | baked or broiled chicken |
| **Dash** | | parsley or basil |
| | | Tomato **slices** |
| **Additional** | | Parmesan **to taste** |

Using a fork, blend oil, vinegar, cheese, and mustard in a bowl. Spoon the mixture over the chicken, top with parsley or basil and tomato slices, and microwave until warm. Top with additional Parmesan, if you like.

# Chickenchiladas

*Do not despair if there are no tortillas in the cafeteria. Just make pita tortillas—cut a piece of pita bread around the edges to make two circles.*

| | | |
|---:|---|---|
| **3/4** | **bowl** | chicken pieces, cut from the bone and chopped |
| **Lots** | | of taco sauce |
| **2** | | tortillas or 1 pita pocket, cut into 2 pita tortillas |
| **Several** | **handfuls** | shredded cheese |
| | | Chopped black olives (optional) |

Pile chicken and a few spoonfuls of taco sauce in the center of each tortilla. Roll each one up (secure with toothpick if necessary). Pour more sauce on top, add cheese, and top with black olives, if you like. Microwave until cheese melts. Serve with extra taco sauce.

# Chicken à l'Orange

*Larry's grandma's recipe (for more of Larry's grandma's cooking see page 139, or visit her at home).*

**1** orange
**2 pats** butter
**1 soupspoon** honey
**3 soupspoons** orange juice
**2 soupspoons** crushed croutons (crush in a bowl with the bottom of a glass)

Cut the orange in half. Section one half of the orange in a bowl (see page 61 for how to section an orange). Set the other half of the orange aside. Add butter, honey, orange juice, and croutons to bowl with sectioned orange. Microwave until butter melts, stir, and continue to microwave until hot. Spoon mixture onto chicken and garnish with rings of orange cut from the unused orange half.

# Thanksgiving Turkey

*For anyone who can't make it home for Thanksgiving break.*

**1 soupspoon** orange juice, apple juice, or cranberry juice
**1/2 cup** chopped apple
**1/2 bowl** cranberry sauce
**1 serving** turkey, sliced or on the bone

Add orange juice and apple to cranberry sauce. Stir, microwave until hot, and stir again. Spoon over turkey.

# *Tiffany Talley's Texas Tech Turkey*

*You've probably never used these ingredients in the same place at the same time, but trust Tiffany of Texas Tech—they make a lip-smackin' dish.*

|  |  |  |
|---:|---|---|
| **1** | **soupspoon** | ketchup |
| **A few** | **drops** | Tabasco sauce |
| **1** | **soupspoon** | Worcestershire sauce |
| **1/2** | **glass** | orange juice |
| **1** | **serving** | turkey, sliced or on the bone |

Add the ketchup, Tabasco sauce, and Worcestershire sauce to the orange juice and stir well. Pour over turkey and microwave until hot.

# FISH SHTICK

The recipes in this section are
designed for plain white fish.
Prepare the topping before you get
the fish from the serving line.

**EAT THE SYSTEM**

**S·A·U·C·E·S**

*Our Eat the System Sauces (pages 147-151) will make a fine piece of fish. Prepare your choice of sauce, spread over a serving of fish, and warm up in the microwave.*

You should try:

**Fish with Claudio's Salsa di Pomodoro**
   (page 148)
**Fish with Mushroom Sauce** (page 149)
**Fish with Mustard Sauce** (page150)
**Fish with Sweet and Sour Sauce** (page 150 )
**Fish with Teriyaki Sauce** (page 151)
**Fish with Garlic Butter** (page 151)

# Fish Mornay

*Mornay sauce, a white sauce with Swiss or Parmesan cheese, was probably named after Phillipe de Mornay (1549–1623), a French Huguenot leader. The dictionary didn't say why.*

**2** **heaping soupspoons** sour cream (lower cal: substitute plain yogurt)

**2** **pats** butter

**1** **handful** shredded cheese, 1 slice Swiss cheese, or 3 soupspoons grated Parmesan cheese

**Dash** garlic powder or garlic salt

**1** **serving** plain fish

**Dash** basil or oregano

Combine sour cream, butter, cheese, and garlic in a bowl. Microwave until butter and cheese melt. Stir and pour over fish. Sprinkle with basil or oregano.

# Lemon Glazed Fish

*Similar to **Sweet and Sour Sauce** (see page 150).*

**2** **soupspoons** honey

**2** **soupspoons** lemon juice

**1** **soupspoon** soy sauce

**1** **serving** plain fish

Combine all ingredients except fish in a cup and stir. Microwave until warm and pour over fish.

# Spring Semester Fish Jardiniere

*Topped with a garden of fresh vegetables.*

4 **pats** butter
Several **squirts** lemon juice
1 **teaspoon** parsley
3/4 **bowl** of your favorite raw or cooked vegetables, sliced (zucchini, squash, tomatoes, carrots, onions, peppers, etc.)
1 **serving** plain fish

Add the butter, lemon juice, and parsley to vegetables. Microwave until the butter melts. Stir to coat vegetables with lemon butter. Spoon vegetable mixture over fish.

# Hot Chili Fish

*Much like fish, you won't survive this without water.*

3 **pats** butter
1 **teaspoon** lemon juice
Chili powder, cayenne pepper, or Tabasco sauce **to taste**
1 **serving** plain fish

In a cup, microwave the butter, lemon juice, and spices until the butter melts. Pour over fish.

# *Your Own Tartar Sauce*

Good with plain
fish, fried fish, or
shellfish.

**1/2  cup** mayonnaise
**1  soupspoon** relish

Add relish to mayonnaise and stir well.

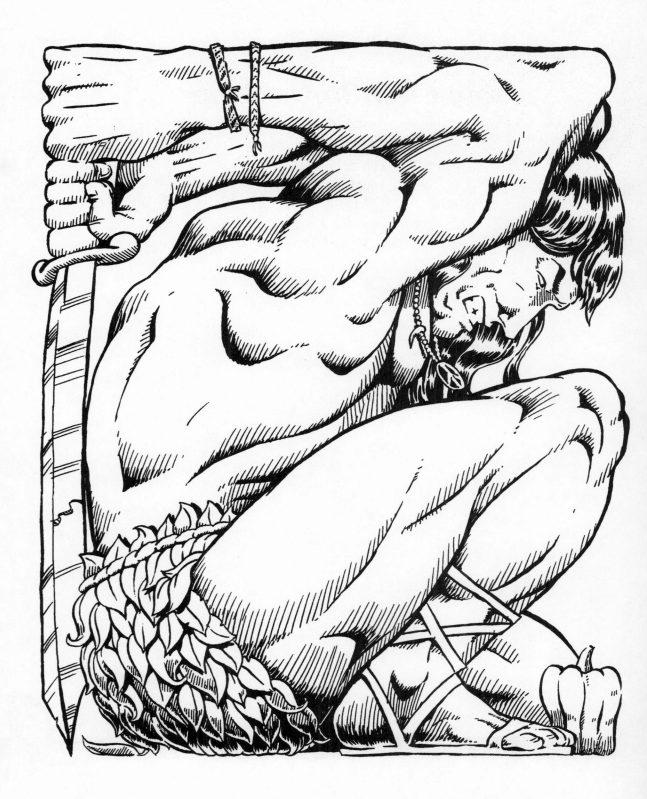

# CONAN
# THE VEGETARIAN:
## *Meatless Options*

These recipes do not contain red meat, chicken, or fish. There are also vegetarian recipes throughout the sandwich, pasta, salad, and side dish sections. Try them all, even if you're not a vegetarian.

# Vegetables with

**EAT THE SYSTEM**

S·A·U·C·E·S

Our Eat the System Sauces (see pages 147-151) will revive salad bar or serving line vegetables. Pour the sauce of your choice over a plate full of your favorites.

We suggest:

**Vegetables with Claudio's Salsa di Pomodoro** (page 148)

**Vegetables with Mustard Sauce** (page 150)

**Vegetables with Teriyaki Sauce** (page 151)

**Vegetables with Garlic Butter** (page 151)

Try these recipes on top of rice, pasta, or toasted bread.

# *Pita Fajitas*

*According to our sources in Palo Alto, the birthplace of this recipe, "Avocado is a staple at Stanford."*

**1** large pita bread (makes two fajitas)
**1** **cup** chopped tomatoes
**1** **cup** chopped green peppers
**1** **cup** chopped onions
**1** **cup** taco sauce
**2** **handfuls** shredded cheese, more if you like
Garnish: avocado slices, sour cream, black olives, Tabasco sauce

With a knife, split the pita carefully around its circumference to make two flat circles.  Place half of the tomatoes, peppers, onions, and taco sauce in the center of each pita.  Roll up each pita (secure with a toothpick if necessary).  Spread the cheese evenly over both pitas.
Microwave until the cheese melts.  Top with avocados, sour cream, olives, and/or Tabasco sauce.

**Note**: For a more elaborate recipe, you can make *Tabasco Tomatoes* (page 134), roll them inside the pita, and melt cheese on top as directed.

# Tabasco Tomatoes

*Liz Tennican of Stanford suggests eating these tomatoes on top of a thick slice of wheaty bread.*

| | | |
|---:|---|---|
| **1** | **soupspoon** | chopped green peppers |
| **1** | **soupspoon** | chopped onions |
| **1/2** | **bowl** | chopped tomatoes |
| **1** | **soupspoon** | salad oil, olive oil if available |
| **1** | **soupspoon** | vinegar |
| **As many** | **drops** | of Tabasco sauce as you dare |

Combine the peppers and onions with the tomatoes.  In a separate glass, mix the oil and vinegar thoroughly, adding Tabasco sauce to taste.  Pour the dressing over the tomatoes and stir well.  Microwave until the tomatoes are warm.

# Grinnell Gazpacho

*The North American cafeteria version of the soup from southern Spain— although it's almost too thick and crunchy to call it soup.*

| | | |
|---:|---|---|
| **1/2** | **bowl** | tomato or cream of tomato soup |
| **1/2** | **cup** | chopped green peppers |
| **1/2** | **cup** | chopped raw onion |
| **1/2** | **cup** | chopped tomatoes |
| **1/2** | **cup** | chopped cucumbers |
| **1** | **heaping soupspoon** | sour cream or plain yogurt |

Get the bowl of soup first so that it can cool while you chop the vegetables.  Add the vegetables to the soup.  Mix well.  Place the sour cream or yogurt in the center of the bowl.

# Cheesi Chili Rice

Beans and rice are excellent complementary proteins (see Appendix IV, Nutrition Erudition, page 181). Kidney beans show up in the salad bar at most colleges or are served as a vegetable in the hot food line. Resourceful and patient cafeteria chefs will sort out the kidney beans from the three-bean salad at the salad bar.

| | | |
|---|---|---|
| 2 | **soupspoons** | taco sauce |
| 1 | **soupspoon** | sour cream |
| 1/2 | **bowl** | kidney beans |
| 1 | **serving** | rice |
| 1 | **handful** | cheese |

Add taco sauce and sour cream to kidney beans and stir well. Spoon mixture over rice and toss cheese on top. Microwave until the cheese melts.

# Ratatouille

A traditional French vegetable stew.

| | | |
|---|---|---|
| 1 | **handful** | chopped eggplant, if available |
| 1 | **handful** | chopped onions |
| 1 | **handful** | or 3/4 cup zucchini, raw or cooked |
| 1 | **soupspoon** | oil, olive oil if available |
| **Dash** | | oregano |
| **Dash** | | garlic salt or garlic powder |
| 1/2 | **bowl** | chopped tomatoes |

Place all ingredients in bowl with tomatoes. Stir and microwave until mixture is thoroughly hot and tomatoes have cooked down enough to make a juice. Stir again. Serve with rice, if desired.

# Tofu with

## EAT THE SYSTEM

## S·A·U·C·E·S

Our Eat the System Sauces (pages 147-151) are definitely good company for tofu. Prepare the sauce of your choice, pour over plain tofu, and warm in microwave if you like.

How about:

TOFU Recipes

## Recipes with Tofu

Most hip college salad bars now include tofu. Tofu is a bean derivative that is exceptionally high in protein and low in fat and cholesterol.

Tofu succumbs easily to peer pressure. Since it has no strong taste of its own, it takes on the taste of its companion. Tofu has the potential to be delicious, if you encourage it to hang out in the right crowd.

# Tofu Étoufée

*Assistant MIT Dean Les Perelman reinvented this classic New Orleans dish in honor of one of Louisiana's few Cajun vegetarians, his former student Eric Lormand (Tulane '86, MIT '90, now assistant professor of philosophy at the University of Michigan). This recipe loses something in the translation from the bayou to the cafeteria, namely, the flour necessary to make a roux (the butter and flour base of an étouffée)—but we've tried to work around that.*

| | |
|---|---|
| **15** | **pats** butter |
| **1** | **handful** celery, chopped small |
| **1** | **handful** onions, chopped small |
| **1** | **handful** green peppers, chopped small |
| **Lots** | of parsley |
| **1/2** | **bowl** tofu cubes |
| | Cayenne pepper **to taste** |
| | Salt **to taste** |

Put butter pats in bowl and melt in microwave. Add celery, onions, green peppers, and parsley. Microwave, stirring a few times during cooking, until the butter starts to brown. Add tofu and microwave again, very briefly. Stir and add cayenne pepper and salt to taste.

# Tofu Curry

*This tofu picks up a bright yellow color from the curry.*

**3** **soupspoons** plain yogurt
**1** **teaspoon** curry powder
**1** **teaspoon** honey
**1** **handful** raisins
**1** **handful** grated or chopped carrot
**3/4** **bowl** tofu cubes

Mix the yogurt, curry powder, honey, raisins, and carrots in a bowl. Add the tofu and stir. Microwave until hot. Serve over rice, if you like.

# Tofu Enchiladas

*Do not despair if there are no tortillas in the cafeteria. Just make pita tortillas—cut a piece of pita bread around the edges to make two circles.*

**2** tortillas or 1 pita pocket cut into 2 pita tortillas
**3/4** **bowl** chopped tofu
**Lots** of taco sauce
**Several** **handfuls** shredded cheese
Chopped black olives (optional)

Pile tofu and a few spoonfuls of taco sauce in the center of each tortilla. Roll each one up (secure with toothpick if necessary). Pour more sauce on top, add cheese, and top with black olives, if you like. Microwave until cheese melts. Serve with extra taco sauce.

# Tofu Parmesan

*Some grandparents may have missed out on the tofu experience—but not Larry's grandmother. She made him this recipe when she visited him at college.*

| | | |
|---:|:---|:---|
| **3** | **heaping** | soupspoons Parmesan cheese |
| **3/4** | **bowl** | crushed croutons (crush them in a bowl with the bottom of a glass) |
| **8** | **pats** | butter |
| **Several** | **dashes** | garlic salt or garlic powder |
| **3/4** | **bowl** | cubed tofu |

Add Parmesan cheese to croutons.  In a separate bowl, melt the butter in the microwave.  Dip each tofu cube in melted butter and roll in croutons and cheese mixture until coated.  Microwave coated cubes of tofu until hot.

# 'ZA:
## Living on Pizza

In a cookbook for college eaters, pizza deserves a chapter all its own.

Unless otherwise noted, you can use the bread of your choice as the "dough": pita bread, French bread, slices of bread, bagels, English muffins, etc. "1 plate" means the amount of bread—1 layer—that fits on a dinner plate.

# 'ZA

Experiment with
your own topping
ideas and
combinations.

For each slice:

**1 plate** of bread

**1 serving** *Claudio's Salsa di Pomodoro* (page 148), or

2/3 bowl prepared tomato sauce

**1 large handful** shredded cheese or several slices cheese

**Any** of the toppings suggested

Toast the bread.  Spoon tomato sauce onto the toast and top with cheese.  Put a handful of suggested toppings on top of the cheese.  Microwave until the cheese bubbles.

Suggested pizza toppings:
chopped mushrooms - chopped red or green peppers - chopped onions - chopped broccoli - chopped or grated carrots - chopped olives - tuna - grated cheese - feta cheese - pineapple - chopped bacon or bacon bits - chopped ham - chopped roast beef - chopped hamburger pieces - hot dog slices

# "Wet Garlics"

A tradition on the Cornell University campus. The legendary Johnny's Hot Truck parks every night at midnight behind the freshman dorms and serves these amazing garlic bread pizzas to hordes of students.

**1 serving** *Greased Lightning Garlic Bread* (page 75)
**1 serving** *Claudio's Salsa di Pomodoro* (page 148) or 3/4 bowl prepared tomato sauce
**2 handfuls** cheese

Spoon the tomato sauce on the garlic bread. Top with cheese. Microwave until the cheese bubbles.

# Pizza Bianco

Naples Pizza in New Haven added this upscale, sauceless pizza to their menu right about when they installed their high-tech video jukeboxes.

**1** pita bread
**1 soupspoon** olive oil or salad oil, or 2 pats butter
**1 handful** grated or shredded cheese, any kind
**1 handful** pizza toppings
**Dashes** garlic powder or garlic salt, oregano, pepper

Toast the pita without cutting it open. Spread the oil on it, still without cutting it. Evenly distribute the cheese and then the pizza toppings on top of the pita. Sprinkle with garlic, oregano, pepper. Microwave until the cheese bubbles.

# *Pesto Pizza*

*A gorgeous green pizza.*

**1 plate** of bread of your choice
**2 heaping soupspoons** chopped basil
**1 soupspoon** grated Parmesan cheese
**Dash** garlic powder or garlic salt
**Several dashes** salt
**3 soupspoons** oil, olive oil if available, or 8 pats butter, melted in the microwave
**2 handfuls** shredded cheese

Toast the bread. Combine basil, Parmesan cheese, garlic, and salt in a bowl. Add oil or melted butter slowly, while stirring. Microwave mixture until oil is hot. Spread the pesto mixture on the bread. Cover with cheese. Microwave until cheese starts to bubble.

# Popeye 'Za

*"I'm strong to the finish / Cuz my 'za has spinach . . ."*

**1** **plate** of bread of your choice
**Several** leaves raw spinach, torn into small pieces
**2** **soupspoons** Olive Oyl
**A few** **dashes** salt
**2** **handfuls** cheese
**A few** black olives, sliced
Black pepper **to taste**

Toast the bread.  Combine spinach, olive oil, and salt in a bowl.  Spread over toast.  Cover with cheese.  Microwave until cheese bubbles.  Garnish with black olives and season with black pepper.

# EAT THE SYSTEM
## S·A·U·C·E·S

We've given these six simple
sauces a chapter of their own
because of their universal appeal.
They can be put on anything—
meats, tofu, poultry, fish, and even
rice or pasta. Just heat the sauce
in the microwave, stir, pour it over
your entree, and warm the whole
thing up once again, if you like. If
you have these recipes at your
forktips, the cafeteria menu will
never catch you off guard.

# Claudio's Salsa di Pomodoro

(Claudio's Tomato Sauce)

*Claudio Cambon was famous around Yale for his Italian cooking. The carrots are Claudio's secret ingredient, but if you don't see them already shredded at the salad bar, you can leave them out. "Never use basil and oregano in the same sauce," says Claudio.*

| | | |
|---|---|---|
| 3 | **soupspoons** | oil, olive oil, if available |
| A few | **dashes** | garlic powder |
| 1 | **handful** | chopped onions |
| A few | **dashes** | basil or oregano |
| 2/3 | **bowl** | tomatoes, chopped small |
| 1 | **small** | handful shredded carrots |
| 1 | **pat** | butter |
| 1 | **teaspoon** | sugar |
| A few | **dashes** | salt and pepper |
| Any | | of the following: chopped green pepper, spicy red pepper, chopped ham |

Grated Parmesan cheese **to taste**

Combine the oil, garlic, onions, and basil or oregano in a bowl and microwave until the oil is hot and the onions have begun to soften. Add the remaining ingredients to the oil mixture and stir well. Microwave again until thoroughly hot. The longer you cook the sauce, the softer the tomatoes will be. "It's a matter of taste," says Claudio.

If you're used to store-bought tomato sauce, keep in mind that Claudio's will not be as smooth and solid red; it will have the authentic tomatoey texture of homemade sauce.

# Barbecue Sauce

| | | |
|---:|:---|:---|
| 1/2 | **bowl** | ketchup |
| 1 | **soupspoon** | mustard |
| 1 | **soupspoon** | vinegar |
| 1 | **soupspoon** | Worcestershire sauce |
| 1 | **soupspoon** | honey |
| A few | **drops** | Tabasco sauce |

Combine everything in a bowl and microwave until hot.  Stir well.

# Mushroom Sauce

| | | |
|---:|:---|:---|
| 2 | **pats** | butter |
| 2 | **soupspoons** | soy sauce |
| Dashes | | oregano, black pepper, and garlic powder |
| 1/2 | **bowl** | chopped mushrooms |

Add the butter, soy sauce, and herbs and spices to the mushrooms.  Microwave until the butter melts.  Stir until blended and microwave again until quite hot, so that the mushrooms have a chance to absorb the sauce.

# Mustard Sauce

1 **soupspoon** mustard
1 **teaspoon** honey
1/2 **glass** sour cream (lower cal: substitute plain yogurt)

Combine mustard and honey with sour cream. Microwave until hot.

# Sweet and Sour Sauce

3 **soupspoons** mustard (2 soupspoons if you use Dijon mustard)
3 **soupspoons** orange marmalade
1 **soupspoon** soy sauce
1 **soupspoon** orange juice
Several **squirts** lemon juice
Pineapple chunks, if available

Combine all ingredients in a bowl. Microwave until hot and stir well. Be sure the honey is thoroughly blended.

# Teriyaki Sauce

|   | | |
|---|---|---|
| **3** | **soupspoons** | soy sauce |
| **1** | **teaspoon** | lemon juice |
| **1 or 2** | **dashes** | ginger |
| **1 or 2** | **dashes** | garlic powder |
| **1** | **teaspoon** | sugar |

Combine all ingredients in a bowl and microwave until hot. Stir well, making sure that sugar is completely dissolved.

# Garlic Butter

|   | | |
|---|---|---|
| **8** | **pats** | butter |
| **Several** | **dashes** | garlic powder or garlic salt |
| **Several** | **dashes** | parsley |

Combine all ingredients in a bowl and microwave until the butter melts. Stir well.

# At finals
## Desserts That Will Destroy the Curve

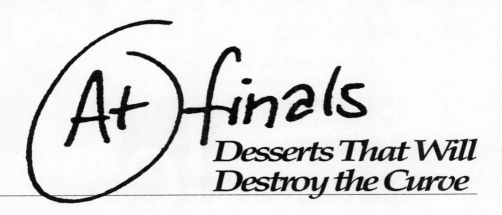

*Now that you're on your own at college, "No dessert until you eat your vegetables" is a thing of the past.*

# The Edible Complex

## Ice Cream Dreams and Their Freudian Interpretations

• *If your cafeteria offers hot fudge sauce, use it as a sublimation for chocolate syrup in any of the following recipes.*

Fig. 18-1

## The Super Eggo

*Make this waffle sundae at brunch, when you're most likely to find both waffles and ice cream. (Some schools, such as Bard College, U. Chicago, and U.C. Santa Cruz offer fresh waffles right off the iron, either made-to-order or make-your-own.)*

|      |                                          |
|------|------------------------------------------|
| 2    | scoops ice cream, the flavor(s) of your choice |
| 1    | waffle, warmed or toasted                |
| Lots | of chocolate syrup                       |
| 1    | banana, apple, or pear, cut in pieces    |
|      | Whipped cream (optional)                 |

Put the ice cream on the waffle. Swirl the chocolate sauce over the ice cream. Top with fruit and with whipped cream, if you like.

## Banana Split Personality

*If you really mean business, you'll make this the real way, with the proper ice cream flavors and their proper toppings. Lynn had a summer job at an old-fashioned ice cream parlor, so she knows what she's talking about.*

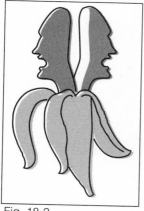

Fig. 18-2

2  soupspoons pineapple chunks, with their juice
2  soupspoons chocolate syrup
2  soupspoons strawberry jam
1  scoop vanilla ice cream
1  scoop chocolate ice cream
1  scoop strawberry ice cream
1  banana, split in half lengthwise
   Whipped cream
   Chopped nuts (optional)

Put the pineapple, chocolate syrup, and strawberry jam in separate cups and microwave each until hot. Meanwhile, place the ice cream scoops together in a bowl and bend the banana halves around the edges.

Put the pineapples on the vanilla ice cream, the chocolate syrup on the chocolate ice cream, and the strawberry jam on the strawberry ice cream. Cover with whipped cream and sprinkle with nuts, if you like. Eat the whole thing yourself when the coast is clear.

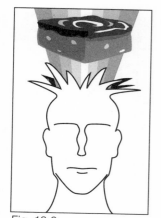

Fig. 18-3

## The Unrepressed Brownie Sundae

*This is the classic brownie sundae. However, Dr. Freud allows for the urge to use a different flavor ice cream or a different sauce (try Peanut Envy, page 157; Mandarin Chocolate, page 161; or Chocolate Raspberry, page 161).*

>     1  brownie
>  Lots  of chocolate syrup
>     2  scoops vanilla ice cream
>        Whipped cream (optional)

Microwave brownie and chocolate syrup separately until hot. Scoop ice cream onto brownie and top with chocolate syrup. Add whipped cream, if you like.

**Cappuccino Brownie Sundae**
Follow directions for Unrepressed Brownie Sundae, using coffee ice cream and topping sundae with a dash of cinnamon.

---

### All Mixed Up
*This is the cafeteria equivalent of the "mix-ins" or "blend-ins" made popular by trendy ice cream parlors.*

>     2  scoops ice cream, the flavor(s) of your choice
>     4  soupspoons of mix-in options: crushed Oreos,
>        crushed cookies, chocolate syrup, peanut
>        butter, raisins, M&Ms, nuts, chocolate chips,
>        chocolate sprinkles, shredded coconut,
>        chopped fruit, etc.

Fig. 18-4

Put ice cream in a bowl. Add mix-in(s). Using one spoon in each hand, fold the mix-in into the ice cream.

Fig. 18-5

### Peanut Envy Chocolate Sauce

*Everyone will want some.*

2 soupspoons peanut butter
1/3 bowl of chocolate syrup
1 serving ice cream of your choice

Add peanut butter to chocolate syrup.  Microwave until warm and soft enough to blend.  Stir and pour over ice cream while still hot.

Fig. 18-6

### Rorschach Shake

*Pour some on the table and tell us what you see.*

3 soupspoons milk
3 teaspoons chocolate syrup
1/2 glass ice cream, the flavor of your choice

Add milk and chocolate syrup to ice cream and stir until smooth enough to drink.

# HOT VANNA BANANAS

*Be sure you know how many n's are in "banana."*

**PEELS OF FORTUNE**

**1** banana
Juice of 2 lemon wedges
**1 teaspoon** sugar
**A few dashes** cinnamon
Vanilla ice cream (low cal: skip the ice cream)

Peel the banana and cut crosswise into circles. Put the banana circles in a bowl and add lemon juice, sugar, and cinnamon. Heat in microwave until mixture is very hot and bananas have softened. Stir well. You can have this dessert on account, on a gift certificate, or on vanilla ice cream.

## Carnegie Melon (low cal)

*A delicious, original taste combination.*

**1 dash** ginger
**1 teaspoon** sugar, powdered if available
**1** cantaloupe **wedge**

Using a fork, thoroughly blend ginger and sugar in a cup. Sprinkle gingerly over cantaloupe wedge.

# Apple Brown Betty

*Made by Tracy Raymond at Brown University, this recipe is otherwise known as Apple Brown Tracy.*

**3/4   bowl** sliced apples (or peaches or pears)
**5 or 6   soupspoons** granola
**1 or 2   pats** butter
**1   teaspoon** sugar, brown sugar if available
Vanilla ice cream (optional)

Cover fruit with granola. Cut butter pats into small pieces and distribute evenly on top of granola. Sprinkle sugar on top. Microwave until the butter and sugar melt and the fruit underneath is hot. Top with vanilla ice cream, if you like.

# Franklin and Marshall Fruit and More

*Courtesy of Nancy Tobin of F & M.*

**1/2   bowl** plain yogurt
**1   soupspoon** fruit juice of your choice
**1   soupspoon** honey
**Dash   cinnamon**
**1   serving** *Frosh Fruit Salad* (page 60), or 1 bowl chopped fruit(s) of your choice
Granola and/or shredded coconut (optional)

Combine yogurt, fruit juice, honey, and cinnamon in a bowl. Pour over fruit salad. Top with granola or coconut, if you like.

# Chocolate Fondue

*Start dipping
immediately.*

Food for dipping: chunks of bread, apple slices, pear slices, banana slices, orange sections, pineapple chunks, peach slices, brownies, cake, etc.

1 **heaping** soupspoon sour cream
1 **soupspoon** hot coffee
2 **soupspoons** cream
3 **pats** butter
1/2 **bowl** chocolate syrup

Prepare a large plate heaped with food for dipping and enough forks to go around.
Add sour cream, coffee, cream, and butter to chocolate syrup. Microwave until the butter melts, stir, and microwave again until very hot.

# German Chocolate Cake

*Lynn's roommate
Paula made this for
her German class
one day. Paula got
an A in German.*

4 **pats** butter
2 **teaspoons** brown sugar
2 **teaspoons** chopped nuts, any kind, or granola
2 **teaspoons** shredded coconut
1 **piece** unfrosted chocolate cake

Combine butter, brown sugar, nuts, and coconut in a cup and microwave until butter melts. Stir well. Spoon mixture on top of the cake. Microwave it again just enough to warm up the cake.

# You Look Marble-ous

*So simple—made with the puddings served for dessert.*

**1 serving** chocolate pudding
**1 serving** butterscotch pudding

Spoon chocolate pudding and then butterscotch pudding into an empty bowl. Run the blade of a knife through it in circles a few times to "marbleize."

# Topping Temptation

*For all recipes, combine ingredients in a cup, microwave until hot, and stir well. Pour in decadent quantities over ice cream, plain cake, or brownies.*

## • Chocolate Raspberry Sauce

**3 soupspoons** chocolate syrup
**2 soupspoons** raspberry jam
**1 soupspoon** cream

## • Cappuccino Sauce

**3 soupspoons** chocolate syrup
**2 soupspoons** hot coffee
**2 dashes** cinnamon

## • Mandarin Chocolate Sauce

**3 soupspoons** chocolate syrup
**2 soupspoons** orange marmalade or apricot jam

## Decadent Goodies

# Pie Beta Kappa

*Serve with honors.*

**1 slice** pie, any kind
**2 scoops** ice cream, any kind

Warm up the pie in the microwave or toaster oven and top with ice cream.

# As American as Luke Heimer

*Luke, a cafeteria chef at St. John's University in Minnesota, says that melted cheese "makes plain apple pie 100 percent better."*

**1 handful** shredded cheese, Cheddar if available
**1 slice** apple pie

Top apple pie with cheese. Microwave until the cheese melts and the pie filling is warm.

# Smart Cookies

*A sandwich, yes, but not endorsed by Tray Gourmet as an alternative to a balanced lunch.*

**2** cookies, any kind
**1 scoop** ice cream, any kind

Warm cookies in microwave or toaster oven. Scoop ice cream onto one cookie and top with the other.

# S'Mores

*Pretend the toaster oven (or microwave) is a roaring campfire. Sing a few folk songs, if it helps.*

Graham crackers
Chocolate syrup, chocolate chips, or chocolate sprinkles
Marshmallows or Marshmallow Fluff

Spread half of the graham crackers on a plate. Put others aside. Drizzle with chocolate syrup, or top with chocolate chips or chocolate sprinkles. Top with marshmallows. Toast or microwave until the marshmallows and chocolate start to melt. Make sandwiches by topping with remaining graham crackers.

# Rice Pudding

*Naples Pizza restaurant doesn't give out their recipe (see page 28), so we figured out how to make rice pudding ourselves.*

**One** of the following: 1 Jello Pudding Pop, 3 heaping soupspoons vanilla pudding, 3 heaping soupspoons vanilla yogurt, 3 heaping soupspoons plain yogurt plus 1 soupspoon honey
**3/4 bowl** cooked rice
**1 small** handful raisins
**Several dashes** cinnamon

If you are using a Pudding Pop, put it in a bowl and microwave it until melted (remove stick after pop melts).
Spoon the melted Pudding Pop, vanilla pudding, or yogurt over the rice. Add raisins and cinnamon, and stir. Microwave until thoroughly hot.

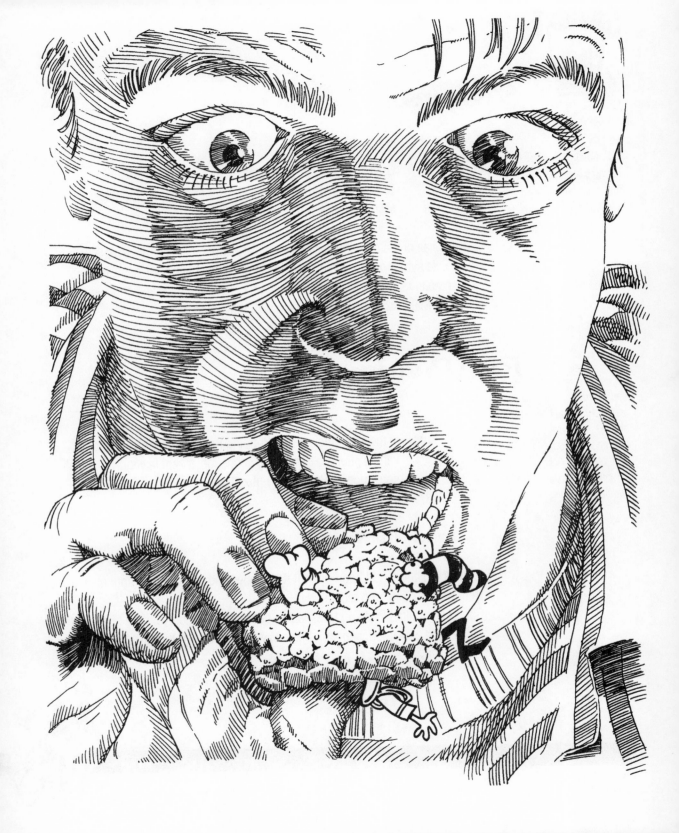

# Rice Krispie Treats

*The treats you never outgrow.*

**2   pats** butter
**1/2   bowl** marshmallows or Marshmallow Fluff
**1/2   bowl** Rice Krispies

Add butter to marshmallows.  Microwave until the butter and marshmallows melt and the mixture is soft enough to stir.  Stir to mix in butter.  Add Krispies and blend well.  Let cool before eating, if you can stand it.

These treats will not look like the nice neat square treats at bake sales — it will be more like one big Rice Krispie Treat lump, which you can eat with a spoon or with your fingers.

## Variations

• Add to the marshmallows before microwaving one or more of the following: 2 soupspoons chocolate syrup, 2 soupspoons peanut butter, 1 handful chocolate chips or chocolate sprinkles, 1 handful shredded coconut, 1 handful raisins.
• Use granola instead of Rice Krispies.

# Beverages
## YOU'D WANT TO SHOTGUN
### IF THEY CAME IN A CAN

*No need to designate a driver.*

# Spelman Spritzer

*A cool drink for hot days in Atlanta.*

**1/2**  **glass** fruit juice, any kind
**1/2**  **glass** carbonated water
**Several**  **squirts** lemon juice

Add fruit juice to carbonated water. Add lemon juice and twist of lemon, if you like.

# Zach's Fresh Squeeze

*Larry's roommate Zach is the best Nerf basketball player in the universe. Teams of ten people have challenged him to full-court Nerf. He has never lost. Many sports experts link Zach's skill to the practice he gets every morning handling oranges. He has developed the following trick for making fresh-squeezed orange juice in the cafeteria. It works with grapefruits as well.*

**Several**  oranges, sliced in half as you would slice a grapefruit
**1**  bowl
**2**  **glasses** (standard institutional-style with bumpy bottoms, if available)

Put one glass upside down in the bowl. Place one orange half flat side down on the bottom of the glass. Press down hard with the palm of your hand and rotate the orange left and right so that the juice drips down the outside of the glass. Repeat with all orange halves until you have as much juice as you want. Remove the glass from the bowl and pour juice into the clean glass.

**Note:** Be gentle – don't shatter the glass with your morning's first rush of adrenalin.

# M.I. Tea Punch

*Refreshes after an afternoon at the lab.*

**1/2** **glass** unsweetened iced tea
**1/2** **glass** fruit juice of your choice

Add juice to iced tea and stir.

# S. A. Tea (Spiced Apple Tea)

*800 Simplicity, 800 Flavor.*

**1/2** **cup** apple juice
**Dash** cinnamon
**1/2** **cup** hot tea

Add apple juice and cinnamon to tea and microwave until mixture is hot.

# *Bloody William and Mary*

We suggest preparing this drink for people in your English History class.

| | | |
|---|---|---|
| **A few** | **squirts** | lemon juice |
| **A few** | **drops** | Tabasco sauce |
| **A few** | **drops** | Worcestershire sauce |
| **1** | **glass** | tomato juice or V-8, not quite full |
| **1** | | celery stalk taller than the glass |

Add the lemon juice, Tabasco sauce, and Worcestershire sauce to the tomato juice.  Stir well with the celery stalk and leave it in for garnish.

# Iced Coffee

*A cool way to answer the call of caffeine, brought to us by Thatcher Zuse of Emory University. He strongly recommends it for "the last thing you drink before you drive home."\**

| | |
|---|---|
| **1** | **teaspoon** instant coffee |
| | Sugar **to taste** (optional) |
| **1** | **soupspoon** hot water |
| **Several** | ice cubes |
| **3/4** | **glass** cold water |
| | Cream or milk **to taste** (optional) |

Put instant coffee and sugar, if used, in a glass. Add hot water and stir until coffee and sugar are dissolved. Add ice cubes, cold water, and cream, if you like, and stir well.

# CJ's Sneaky Cocoa

*Colin J. Lingle of Yale made this specialty for people who said the magic word.*

| | |
|---|---|
| **2** | **teaspoons** instant cocoa |
| **3/4** | **glass** hot coffee |
| **1** | **soupspoon** cream or milk, or whipped cream, if available |
| **Dash** | cinnamon |

Add cocoa to coffee and stir until dissolved. Stir in milk or top with whipped cream. Sprinkle cinnamon on top.

\*Speaking of caffeine, Thatcher also told us how Emory students combat the high price of soda in their cafeterias: It's called The Double Coke. You fill up a glass with Coke from the soda fountain and put it on your tray. Then you get a can of Coke from the cooler. You open the can of Coke and put it next to your glass. The cashier will think you have simply poured some of the Coke from the can into your glass.

Beverages

# Matt Heimer's Root Beer Float

*Grandma Heimer used to make Matt this treat, but once he went off to make his own at Yale, she had no way of stopping him from having seconds, thirds, and fourths.*

**1 scoop** vanilla ice cream (vanilla is standard, chocolate chip is Matt's favorite variation)

**2/3 glass** root beer

Add ice cream carefully to root beer. Eat with spoon and/or straw.

# New York University Egg Cream

*Funny, there are no eggs in this recipe, but that's the name of this old New York soda fountain standby.*

**1 soupspoon** chocolate syrup

**1/4 glass** milk or cream

**3/4 glass** carbonated water

Add chocolate syrup to milk and stir until you have chocolate milk. Add carbonated water and stir well.

To make a classic ice cream soda, add a scoop or two of ice cream (you'll have to plan ahead and leave room in the glass).

# Café au Lait
## or Café con Leche
### or Kahawa Pamoja Maziwa
#### or Coffee with Milk

*. . . depending on what language you've used to fulfill your foreign language requirement.*

- The closest-to-authentic way

  **1/2** **cup** milk (preferably whole milk)
  **1/2** **cup** hot coffee (in a separate cup)
  **1** empty coffee cup
  Sugar **to taste** (optional)

Heat the milk in the microwave until very hot (check on it frequently to prevent it from boiling).  Pour the hot milk and the hot coffee into the empty cup simultaneously.

If it doesn't all fit, don't worry, just pour in as much as you can until the new coffee is pale brown.  With practice, you can learn to pour in exactly the coffee to milk ratio that you prefer.  Add sugar if you like.

- The way that uses only one coffee cup

  **1** **cup** milk
  **1** **teaspoon** or 1 packet instant coffee
  Sugar **to taste** (optional)

Heat the milk in the microwave as in method 1.  Stir in instant coffee until thoroughly dissolved.  Add sugar if you like.

# APPENDIX I
## Cafeteria Menus for Those Special College Occasions

## Dining-Hall Dating

*A romantic dinner for two in the cafeteria can make for a memorable, impressive, and cheap date. You'll get to show off your grace and culinary prowess, and if you handle it just right, you can make an absurd spectacle of yourself. Tell your date to dress formally for a gourmet meal. And who knows? Maybe your next meal together will be breakfast.*

Suggested menu:

**Beverage** *Spelman Spritzer* (page 168)

**Hors D'Oeuvre** *Fond O'You Cheese Fondue* (page 79)

**Salad** Tossed Salad with *Lemon Vinaigrette* (page 69)

**Entrée** *Bistec Moutard et Champignons* (page 103)

**Bread** *Pa amb Tomaquet* (page 76)

**Dessert** *Chocolate Fondue* (page 160) with peaches for dipping*

**Music** Ask a friend who plays violin, flute, classical guitar, or the bongos to serenade you. Or just use a portable cassette player, or even one Walkman with two sets of headphones. We recommend "If I Said You Had a Beautiful Body, Would You Hold it Against Me?" by the Bellamy Brothers, or a similar work by Tchaikovsky.

**Ambiance** Set the table with two formal place settings (see right diagram). Candlelight is key. Ask your date to dance with you before dinner and between courses. Forget the forks with the fondue — feed it to your date with your fingers (Larry got a date for the formal this way).

*Peaches, along with asparagus, garlic, honey, lobster, and oysters, are believed to be aphrodisiacs. You might want to devise ways of incorporating more of them into your menu.

# The Table:

## Breakfast in Bed

to Smuggle to Your Roommate on His or Her Birthday

Suggested menu:

- *Zach's Fresh Squeeze* (page 168)

- *Cafe au Lait* (page 173)

- *Carnegie Melon* (page 158)

- *Je Ne Sais Quoi Crêpes* with roommate's favorite filling (page 24)

- Have an accomplice distract the manager while you sneak by with the tray.

## Luncheon with the Bridge Club

(if there isn't one already, found one yourself)

Suggested menu:

- *M.I.Tea Punch* (page 169)

- *Courtly Cucumber Sandwiches* (page 44)

- *Waldorf Salad* (page 53)

- *"You Look Marble-ous" Pudding* (page 161)

- Fresh fruit

## Dinner with Your Parents

DO NOT MAKE ANYTHING FROM THIS COOKBOOK.

(See Appendix II, *"Cooking During Parents' Weekend."*)

176

## Big Meal Before the Big Test

The protein and fiber will keep you cranking.

**a**) suggested breakfast menu:

- Fruit juice
- A big glass of milk
- Spread #2 from *A Full Page of Spreads* (page 28)

**b**) suggested lunch menu:

- Fruit juice
- *Spinach Salad* (page 54)
- *Michigan Go Bleu Burger* (page 104)
- Fresh fruit

## Lunch with your Professor

**a**) in a class you're doing well in:

- *Bloody William and Mary* (page 170)
- *Nietzsche's Nachos* (page 73)
- *I Think Therefore I Ham Salad* (page 57), or
- *Multi-Cultural Tuna Salad* (page 59), on a bed of greens
- *Pie Beta Kappa* (page 162)
- *S.A.Tea* (page 169)

**b**) in a class you're not doing so well in:

Follow menu and instructions for *Dining-Hall Dating*, but use forks for the fondue.

# APPENDIX II
## How to Make Good Food Taste Bad:
## Cooking During Parents' Weekend

There are two days each school year when you will not need *Tray Gourmet*. The cafeteria meals during this time are delicious. The ingredients are fresh, and the recipes are inspired.

You'll know something's up even before you get your food. The floors and silverware sparkle; the tables gleam. There are candles; there are flowers. You might suspect that you've bumbled into the world's largest dining-hall date (see Appendix I), were it not for all the people in the cafeteria who are older than you.

These people are parents. It is Parents' Weekend.

If you allow your parents into the cafeteria at this time, they will rave about the food. They will tell you that when they were your age they had to walk twelve miles to the cafeteria during monsoon season for one bowl of gruel. They will tell you how lucky you are.

This reaction is undesirable. If your parents think that you eat well at college—with or without *Tray Gourmet*—they will no longer worry about you eating out there on your own. And if they are not worrying about you, they are not sending you care packages.

What can you do in this emergency?

Reverse the process that you normally follow when you use this cookbook.

That's right. Instead of making your school food into cool food, you now have to make the cool food into school food. It's for your own good.

178

# APPENDIX II
## *Reverse Care Packages:*
## *Goodies to Send Home*

Send cafeteria goodies home to your parents in the same tins they have used for their own care packages. This way, your parents will feel obliged to fill 'em up and send 'em back.

We suggest sending:
- *German Chocolate Cake* (page 160)
- *Rice Krispie Treats* (page 165)
- *S'Mores* (page 163)

# APPENDIX IV
## *Was It Good For You?*
## *Nutrition Erudition*
## *Topic 1: Collegiate Body Abuse*

*Many activities associated with college—sports, parties, all-nighters—can make "the best years of your life" the roughest years for your body. College students tend to make a lot of cruel and unusual demands on their bodies without always giving them a healthy diet in return. What follows are the answers to questions students ask—or should be asking—about their health and nutrition during college. If a question of yours is not answered here, ask at the cafeteria; most colleges employ dieticians to make sure that the meal plans are healthy.*

## • *What does caffeine do to me?*

Caffeine is one drug to which few college students say no. It induces a state known as a "caffeine high," which supposedly helps students stay awake in morning classes or in wee hour cram jams. The nature of this high varies a great deal from person to person. Some people get completely strung out while others show almost no response.

Physiologically, caffeine raises the heart rate, stimulates the gastrointestinal tract, and releases adrenaline-like substances into the blood. The peak of the caffeine high is usually felt 1 to 4 hours after ingestion. If you consume caffeine on an empty stomach you will feel it sooner and probably more intensely than if you consume it with a meal. The caffeine high can last for as long as four hours.

The bitter irony of "doing caffeine" is that you'll feel even more tired when you come down from the high. Also, because caffeine stimulates the digestive tract, it can cause the "caffeine munchies." The resulting food run may take as much time away from your studying as a refreshing catnap. In extremely large quantities, however, caffeine tends to suppress hunger because it may make you literally too nervous to eat. Caffeine also causes headaches and nausea in some people. There is not yet large-scale scientific consensus on any detrimental long-term effects of caffeine. Some studies have found a link between regular caffeine intake and slightly

decreased fertility in women; questions have been raised as to whether drinking decaffeinated beverages is actually any healthier than drinking caffeinated ones. Do not take this lack of consensus to be your license to chug coffee by the gallon. To this day, no respected researcher has come forward to advocate saturating your body with stimulants.

### • How can I get rid of this hangover?

Hangovers hit you when the by-products of ethanol and other chemicals contained in alcoholic beverages metabolize in your system. They are accompanied by a general dehydration of the body.

If there were an all-purpose hangover cure, somebody would be very, very rich. But here are two things that may decrease the agony:

1. Drink lots of water before you go to bed to prevent dehydration.
2. Consume sugar the next morning. A big glass of fruit juice should give you

the necessary sugar to help metabolize the chemicals that are causing the hangover.
3. Some say eating a banana (high in potassium) also helps.

### • What should I eat at dinner to help me stay awake during an all-nighter?

High-protein foods are the best for pulling you through all-nighters. Unlike starches and sugars, they do not tend to make you sleepy. A good meal for the dinner before an all-nighter might include: meat, milk, cheese, beans with a starch (this combination forms a protein), or peanut butter, as well as some fruits and vegetables. You should also stick to midnight snacks with protein such as cheese and peanut butter. The classic study sustenance of cookies and chips will only make you drowsy. If you must eat something to fulfill the chip-type food craving, try hot air-popped popcorn.

### • Is it okay that I usually skip breakfast?

From a nutritional perspective, no, it is not okay. From an "I have an Organic Chemistry midterm at 8:30 AM and I haven't bought the book yet" perspective, it is easy to see things a little differently.

We do realize that sometimes during college, deciding whether to eat, sleep, or cram is not a matter of nutritional concern; it is a matter of survival. But don't let skipping breakfast become a habit. It's easy enough to grab a piece of fruit on the run to get something in your system. Eating nothing at all confuses your metabolism and may impair your ability to concentrate in class.

If eating breakfast makes you feel sleepy, try eating less sugar (in cereals and pastries) and more fiber or protein (in peanut butter, wheat bread, milk, or yogurt).

**183**

# Topic 2: Nutrition for Athletes

## • What special eating habits should athletes acquire?

The nutritional breakdown for athletes recommended by the ADA (American Dietetic Association) suggests that an athlete's caloric intake should be: 60 to 70 percent carbohydrates, 10 to 12 percent protein, and 20 to 30 percent fat.

Eat plenty of complex carbohydrates (starches), a good source of energy. Stay away from simple carbohydrates (sugars). Make sure you are getting enough protein (meats, beans, eggs, dairy products, milk) in order to help build muscle tissue. But remember, you don't build muscle simply by eating protein. If you don't exercise as well, the body converts the protein into fat. Protein supplements and the traditional training meal of big hunks of steak and twenty glasses of milk are completely unnecessary. The protein needs of athletes are only slightly greater than those of non-athletes, and most Americans eat more protein than they need anyway.

Athletes should also be sure to drink a lot of liquids. Keep drinking even after you have satisfied your thirst. On a hot day, a runner can lose a quart of water in half an hour. This kind of dehydration is extremely dangerous for the body and will impair stamina and other physical abilities. So, for the sake of your health and for the sake of your athletic performance, stay hydrated. Gatorade and other "athletic drinks" are no better for you than water and fruit juice.

## • What about carbohydrate loading?

Carbohydrate loading (eating extreme amounts of starches in the days before a competition) used to be recommended by sports nutritionists, but is now generally frowned upon. You should eat plenty of carbohydrates, but it is usually not a good idea to really "load" up on any type of food.

# Topic 3: Dieting

### • How can I lose weight?

The "'I lost 350 pounds in 12 hours with the Amazing New Eel and Oreo Diet,' Raves Marie Osmond's Astrologer" diet plan is the wrong way to lose weight. The only way to lose weight is to eat fewer calories than your body burns. That way, your body starts to burn its own fat in order to make up for the food that you are not eating. The two ways to make this happen are to exercise more, which burns more calories, and to eat less, which decreases your calorie intake.

Exercise contributes to dieting in two stages. First, you burn calories while you are exercising. Then, you build more muscle tissue. The cells in this new muscle tissue need to be fed, so they burn calories even when you are not exercising. When you are stronger, there is more of you to feed and therefore you burn more calories.

### • Do I need to lose weight?

Probably not. See what your doctor recommends.

### • How come I seem to be stuck at this weight whether I diet or not?

Most people find that they have a certain weight that their body likes to maintain. If they diet a lot they don't easily drop below this weight and if they eat a lot they don't easily rise above this weight. This weight is known as a set point. Physiologically, set points exist because the metabolism tries to maintain balance in the body. If you do not eat enough, your metabolism becomes extremely efficient and you do not burn as many calories as you normally would. If you eat too much, your metabolism goes into overdrive and you burn more calories than you normally would.

Some people are lucky and their set points are naturally at the weight that they want to be. Other people are uncomfortable with their set points. The good news is that set points can be changed. If you think your set point is too high, increase your exercise. If you think your set point is lower than your desired weight, it is not recommended that you cut back on exercise, but rather that you eat more food more often. Try eating six smaller meals a day instead of three. Eat a highly caloric—but nutritious—snack before bed.

This information on weight loss and gain is by no means exhaustive. Consult a doctor or weight counselor if you have any more specific questions or concerns.

# Topic 4: Sleeping and Waking

## • What should I do if I am having trouble sleeping?

Try eating more carbohydrates and fruits in the hours before bedtime. Stay away from caffeine. Try to go to sleep and wake up at similar times each day.

## • Why am I always tired during the day?

The obvious answer is that you might not be getting enough sleep. If that's not it, you may want to try cutting down on the amount of sugar you consume. If it's really a serious problem, you might want to consult a doctor.

186

# APPENDIX V
## Growing Your Own Herb Garden

Lynn once made the mistake of inviting one of Larry's less disciplined roommates to one of her more civilized parties. As the evening progressed, Larry's roommate—we'll call him Bart—came to the egalitarian conclusion that houseplants, too, had an inalienable right to get drunk. Bart resolved to teach Lynn's adored greenery how to shotgun a beer. Larry tried to stop him, but there was nothing he could do. Bart said, "Don't worry, Larry, I took their car keys," and proceeded to drink Lynn's last philodendron under the table. Kind, generous, and enterprising co-author that he is, Larry set out the next morning to replace Lynn's permanently hungover flora with some fresh herb plants for them to use in their cafeteria cooking. He bought seeds and supplies at the garden store and we had a garden of fragrant and beautiful herbs in a matter of months. The herbs were a wonderful addition both to Lynn's dorm room and to Lynn and Larry's cafeteria concoctions. Indeed, fresh herbs raise any recipe to new heights of deliciousness and elegance. Whether you are getting serious about cafeteria cooking or you simply want something unusual, fragrant, and legal sprouting in your room, we suggest that you plant an herb garden. While the basic premise of *Tray Gourmet* is that all the needed ingredients are already in the cafeteria, fresh herbs are our one exception. If you give your indoor garden proper care, you can adorn your dinner with a mini-herb harvest every night.

You can get your supplies at a local plant and gardening store, which can be found near even the most urban universities.

### You'll need the following things to get started:

- 1 medium-sized bag of potting soil (regardless of the irony of purchasing additional dirt for your dorm room).

- 1 very small (about 3 inches) plastic pot for each type of herb.

- Individual packages of herb seeds. Oregano, basil, parsley, and dill come up most often in our recipes, but don't hesitate to experiment with herbs like mint, chives, thyme, and rosemary.

- A plastic or aluminum foil tray that can hold all the plastic pots.

- Some plastic wrap or a plastic bag (you can finagle either one from someone behind the scenes in the cafeteria).

### 188

### You'll eventually need:

- 1 clay pot (about 6 inches in diameter) for each type of herb that makes it through the plastic pot stage.

- Several handfuls of pebbles or gravel, or the remnants of the clay pot you dropped.

- One plastic or aluminum foil saucer per clay pot.

- A spray bottle to squirt water on your plant leaves. Buy it at the drugstore, not the plant store — it'll be cheaper.

### You may need:

- Liquid fertilizer. Ask the person at the plant store for the best brand for your herb.

### You do not need:

- A watering can. Just use an empty bottle or soda can.

It is best to start this project right away in the fall or in very early spring so that your babies grow up in as much sunlight as possible. Remember, it may not be your fault if your plants don't make it this time around. You can always start over.

**Fill** each small plastic pot almost to the top with soil. **Sprinkle** a few pinches of herb seeds in each pot. Be absolutely sure to **label** your pots with the name of each herb as you go (use a permanent marker on a piece of clear tape). **Cover** the seeds with a thin layer of additional soil. Put away the extra seeds and soil for later. For now you will have to water your seeds from the bottom up in order to avoid washing them away. **Fill** your plastic or foil tray with one ounce of water, then **set** the pots in and leave them there until the top of the soil is moist. **Watch** carefully— the process does not take very long. You may have to add more water to the tray, but **don't** let the soil get

# PERCY THE PLASTIC POT RELATES THE GROWING OF HERBS

First soil, then a few seeds, then a thin layer of soil

SEED

water from bottom up

Cover to keep in moisture

IN AS LONG AS TWO WEEKS

Uncover when Herb Sprouts

When he's too big for me ...

replant in a larger, clay pot

First pebbles, then soil, then the plant, filling in soil around the sides

Remember to rotate so it gets sun evenly

and spray the leaves every few days

It's fun to thin!

PERCY!

muddy. (If you never did find a tray, you can put the stopper in the sink and water your plants there, but be sure that stray soil doesn't clog the drain.)

**Cover** the entire tray of pots with a sheet of plastic wrap or cover each pot with a plastic bag. The plastic will keep the soil humid.

**Place** the tray in a sunny spot on the windowsill, and wait. On cloudy days leave your desk light on about three to five inches from the pots before you leave for class. Turn the light off at night so your plants will, unlike the average college student, be on a regular night-and-day schedule.

**Remove** the plastic from each pot when you see the seeds inside begin to sprout. It may take as long as two weeks, so don't decide prematurely that you have failed as a greenthumb or make plans to transfer out of the agricultural school.

You'll need to **transplant** your herbs into the clay pots when the plants start to look crowded in the plastic ones. First **place** a layer of pebbles (or clay pot fragments) in the bottom of each pot to help with drainage. Then **add** about an inch of soil on top of the pebbles.

One at a time, **hold** each plastic pot horizontally and tap lightly around the sides until you can **remove** the soil intact in a plastic-pot shaped clump. You may have to poke a thin knife around the edges to loosen the soil. Be extremely careful with each step of this process because the roots are very delicate.

**Place** each clump in the center of a clay pot. **Add** more soil around the edges and, if necessary, underneath the clump, until the pot is full and the clump is stable. The soil should come right up to the top of the pot so that as much light as possible can reach the plants. Be sure not to pack the soil down too tightly. Place each pot in a saucer and put them on a sunny windowsill. You will need to rotate your plants since their light source will be only on one side. When the stalks start leaning one way, **rotate** the opposite side into the lightest area. (If you have an acute shortage of light, a special plant light will do the trick—ask at the plant store.)

**Pay** close **attention** to each plant's individual watering needs.

Keep the soil moist but not muddy. **Pour** water into the pots until some drips out into the saucer below, so you know that the water has reached the roots. **Do not,** however, let the plant sit in a puddle or let unabsorbed water sit on the soil. You should also **spray** the leaves and stems with water every few days to keep them happy and free of dorm dust.

**Thin** each plant (pull off select leaves and stalks) mercilessly so that it doesn't get crowded and compete with itself for sustenance. The cool thing about thinning herbs is that you get to eat what you thin. You can start eating as soon as they are big enough to thin.

Make sure you find someone to herb-sit for you if you leave school for vacation. Give them, along with explicit care and feeding instructions, to a trustworthy friend or professor who lives near campus. Offer the lucky plant-sitter full eating privileges as payment.

## *A few specific hints*

**Basil**  Trim off the blossoms to encourage good foliage.

**Chives**  Trim them regularly. A little liquid fertilizer will produce greener growth. If they look like they're giving out, they just need a little rest. Thin the plant and let it convalesce in the fridge for about two weeks.

**Mint**  Give it good light and frequent baths with the sprayer. Clip off the runners and pinch off the terminal leaf clusters to encourage growth.

**Oregano**  It takes at least two weeks to germinate. Give the stalks plenty of space to spread out.

**Rosemary**  It needs a lot of attention and tender loving care. You may fertilize it sparingly. Spray it with water frequently. Pinch off any pale growth at the tips of the branches. If the leaves start to look yellow, give them more light.

**Thyme**  Make sure it has good drainage. The leaves will always be pretty small, so don't think you're responsible for stunting its growth. Be sure to keep the leaves clean by spraying them with water.

Here are some of our favorite recipes that feature fresh herbs:

### LARRY BERGER

grew up in Ithaca, New York, where he and two high school friends wrote *Up Your Score: The Underground Guide to Psyching Out the SAT* (New Chapter Press, 1987). He graduated summa cum laude in 1990 from Yale, where he won the undergraduate fiction writing competition and the Herson prize for an outstanding student of English. While at Yale, Larry was co-director of the Children in Crisis Big Sibling Program and co-founded Booksgiving, an organization that collects used books from the Yale community for distribution to underprivileged youth.

Larry has received a Rhodes Scholarship for study at Oxford, where he plans to incite a student revolution demanding the installation of microwaves in the 700-year-old dining halls.

Larry spent the year after college writing *Voices from the Hole in the Wall Gang Camp* (Little Brown, 1992).

### LYNN HARRIS

grew up in Lexington, Massachusetts, and went to the Winsor School in Boston, which has a great salad bar. She graduated summa cum laude in 1990 from Yale, where she won the Steve Adams Cup for community service through performing arts, and several prizes for journalistic and academic writing. While at Yale, Lynn tutored New Haven students in English and Spanish and belonged to Something Extra, a women's a cappella singing group. Lynn was chosen as an American Society of Magazine Editors intern in 1989 and is now a freelance writer for various national and trade magazines. She is Vice President for Public Relations for the Boston chapter of the National Organization for Women.

### CHRIS KALB

grew up in Hatboro, Pennsylvania (on the R2 line out of Philly), where he went to public school. He graduated from Yale in 1990 with a degree in graphic design. While at Yale, Chris was Graphics Editor of the Yale Daily News for two years, and led theater workshops with New Haven kids for the Dramat Children's Theater, with whom he also did the occasional play. While trying hard not to become the Next Doonesbury with his strip "P.S.," which appeared in the Yale Daily News, he won the 1988 Charles M. Schulz Award, given to the most promising college cartoonist in the country.

Chris is putting his design degree to good use at Montgomery Publishing, doing newspaper ads in Pennsylvania to support his freelance art habit.